MW01096508

*A Practical Guide to*

# Improve Your Emotional Intelligence At Work & In Relationships

## Shawn Kent Hayashi

*Contributors*:

Kate Early
William Hagan
Emily Hammel-Shaver
Angela Rice
Melanie Sanchez-Jones
Kristy Tan Neckowicz

*Published By:*

THE PROFESSIONAL DEVELOPMENT GROUP LLC

FIRST EDITION

ISBN: 978-1523412167

Cover Design by Suzana Stankovic

Illustrations by Emily Hammel-Shaver

# Also by Shawn Kent Hayashi

*Conversations that Get Results & Inspire Collaboration:*
  *Engage Your Team, Your Peers & Your Manager to Take Action*

*Conversations for Creating Star Performers:*
  *Go Beyond the Performance Review to Inspire Excellence Every Day*

*Conversations for Change®:*
  *12 Ways to Say It Right When It Matters Most*

*Mastering Your Influence™*

*The Influence Journey™*

*Power Presentations: How to Connect with Your Audience &*
  *Sell Your Ideas*

# Contents

Thank you, Jim Hayashi, for being my muse.
I would never have written this book without you.

# Preface

Recently, I met Vanessa. The first thing I noticed was that, like most six-year-old girls, she laughed when playing with puppies and cried when her parents told her she had eaten enough cake. However, unlike most six-year-olds, Vanessa speaks four languages fluently, which filled me with awe.

She never took a course or worked hard at learning the four languages.

I do not speak four languages fluently! Is Vanessa smarter than me? Is her brain more capable than mine even at age six?

No. But she is more capable than I am in speaking four languages. And that's because she had more exposure to more languages than I did.

Yet even though Vanessa has foreign language skills I do not, if I choose, I could acquire the same degree of proficiency. This is true of anyone who chooses to study a foreign language, and makes a consistent effort to practice speaking and listening.

Mastering the language of emotional intelligence is no different. We all possess the capacity for learning it, but that capacity remains dormant until we develop an awareness of this type of literacy and recognize the value in acquiring it.

When we observe a leader who is skilled at connecting with others and bringing out the best in them, we become conscious of "people skills" though we might not know we can acquire those same skills.

Yet, just as we can learn foreign languages – through focused study and determination – we can expand our emotional literacy and improve our own "people skills." Once we abandon the assumption that someone is naturally smarter or innately gifted, we can get down to the business of learning.

Why invest time and energy in raising your emotional intelligence quotient (EQ)? The simple answer is that a higher EQ deepens self-knowledge and improves relationships – whether those relationships are with people at work around the conference table or at home around the kitchen table.

For those of us not lucky enough to have grown up in Vanessa's shoes, the study of language and the development of literacy begins with a book that guides us to practice. And the same thing applies to this book on emotional intelligence. It is unlike any other because it specifically guides you to move from passively reading about improving your emotional intelligence to actually putting it into practice as quickly as possible. Here you'll also read, through real-life stories, how others succeeded in creating better outcomes for themselves using these same exercises. Using this book, you'll complete the Emotions Journal Exercises and be able to watch yourself grow.

Ample research has shown that emotional awareness and self-regulation are the requisite skills for personal happiness and professional success. Plenty of books have presented these concepts and cited the current research, but knowing about emotional intelligence is not enough. The real value is in knowing how to apply it, every day and in all situations, to create and sustain a life filled with joy and passion.

SHAWN KENT HAYASHI

# CHAPTER 1

# Getting Ready to Thrive:
# Becoming Emotionally Literate

Ashley made a great impression on me as I watched her greet each person with a warm hello and a firm handshake. Conversations flowed easily when she was taking part. Sharing stories and asking questions that easily engaged people in meaningful ways, she made her goals clear and spelled out the direction she was headed. As a result, she inspired people to join the adventure she was creating.

Ashley started her own company several years ago and she has attracted a dynamic team of people to work with her. When I met her team, I realized they all shared her infectious excitement about the business and what they were co-creating. Soon I felt the same excitement too! Fun, passion, and creativity were obvious both in private conversations with Ashley and in team meetings. Ashley was thriving in whatever she did.

Meeting Mary was a different experience. Mary looked tired and her half smile caused me to wonder if she was faking cheerfulness. Even later, when we talked on the phone, her voice lifted up briefly in what sounded like an attempt to echo the enthusiasm she had heard in my greeting, but then it quickly flattened into a monotone. During our first conversation concerning a project for her company, she wove in a few details about her life, including her husband not being happy in his work and her daughter about to leave for college. After detailing how our project would flow, she confided that in the span of four years, four members of her family had passed away. It then became clear to me that in dealing with an endless loop of illness, hospitalizations, and death, feeling sad had become a habit for Mary, but she didn't realize it herself.

Mary's sadness made others at work avoid her because it was difficult to get her to laugh or get excited about things. As a result, her own work suffered from lack of motivation and it even affected her ability to make decisions. Mary was stuck in sadness and everyone could see it but her.

## Emotional Awareness

Ashley thrived and Mary withered because of how each of them dealt with their emotions. This difference stemmed directly from their emotional awareness. Whereas Ashley was able to rise above the hardship in her life, Mary couldn't break free. One was a prisoner of her emotions; the other was not.

The difference between Ashley and Mary was not that Ashley had not suffered loss; she had. I later learned that earlier in her career, Ashley experienced both the loss of her dream job and a late-term miscarriage. What's more, because of her husband's career, Ashley had relocated with him to a new part of the country and had to re-establish her career. Yet today she is thriving because her emotional awareness helped her to process her feelings, to channel her emotions into positive actions, and to help her move forward.

Mary, on the other hand, lacked emotional awareness; in fact, she was unaware that she was wallowing in sadness. If she'd realized this fact, she would have been on the first step to getting herself out of it.

Ashley's awareness of her emotional state made her emotionally literate, but Mary's inability to grasp her emotional state made her emotionally illiterate.

## Emotional Literacy

When I first heard the term "emotionally illiterate," it was a lightening bolt moment. I knew instantly that I was emotionally illiterate and I wanted to become emotionally literate – fast! I was asked by the president of the organization in which I worked to help prepare the leadership team for an upcoming, unannounced merger. I thought we needed to develop change management skills on the leadership team. But after bringing in a change management expert to meet with each of the leaders in our company, he said "We can't focus on change management first. We have a bigger issue to deal with. The leaders in this organization are emotionally illiterate. As a result, they will not be able to guide their people and teams through the emotions that will arise during a merger."

I realized in that lightening bolt moment that I wanted to develop my own emotional literacy so that I could help our leadership team to do the same. This meant that I had to start with myself first and become totally aware of what I was feeling, and then use that awareness to consciously guide my own actions.

## Emotional Literacy = Emotional Awareness

To be *literate* means "being able to read and write." To be *emotionally literate* means being able to both read and use your own emotions constructively. We achieve **emotional literacy** by actively reflecting on and learning from all experiences both good and bad, and connecting those experiences to specific emotions.

Beginning this process can be overwhelming as I myself learned when I set out to master emotional literacy. I had decided that the best way to easily identify each type of emotion was to create an emotions dictionary.

When I began identifying words with emotional connotations, I realized that there were more than 3000 to choose from. What initially seemed like a simple task – identifying what I was feeling–turned out to require an inordinate amount of time and focus. When someone asked me what I was feeling, I would become overwhelmed –

which of the 3000 words would I choose from? Then I learned about the seven core emotions and that changed everything.

## The 7 Core Emotions

Dr. Izzy Justice, who has a PhD in Emotional Intelligence, taught me that there are seven core emotions and that each one is quantifiable because of its chemical presence in the body. You could say each emotion has its own "chemical marinade."

Yes, I know, the brilliant Pixar film on emotional intelligence *Inside Out*, which animated the core emotions, only depicted five. Pete Docter, the film's director, consulted with an expert who identified six core emotions. Docter simplified the number of characters in the film by eliminating surprise and focusing the story around joy, sadness, fear, anger and disgust, which worked in the film, but real life is more complex than a movie.

The truth is, scientists have not reached consensus about just how many core emotions there are. Some say there are as many as eight (joy, sadness, trust, disgust, fear, anger, surprise and anticipation) and others say only four (happiness, sadness, anger and fear).

In my work as an executive coach, which usually incorporates emotional intelligence coaching, I have found that Dr. Izzy Justice's list of seven core emotions is a useful guide.

While Justice identifies just seven core emotions, there are dozens of different words and expressions used to describe each of them. Knowing these expressions can be useful in connecting personal experience to each emotion. Let's start by examining descriptions of the seven core emotions so it will be easier for you to identify what you are feeling now.

The seven core emotions are:

1. **Love** – Feeling passionate, cherished, like being on cloud nine or walking on sunshine, euphoric, etc.

2. **Joy** – Feeling blissful, cheerful, good, jubilant, etc.

3. **Hope** – Feeling optimistic, seeing possibilities, confident, etc.

4. **Envy** – Feeling jealous, resentful, a yearning, etc.

5. **Sadness** – Feeling lonely, hollow, alienated, depressed, numb, etc.

6. **Anger** – Feeling annoyed, bitter, frustrated, resentful, etc.

7. **Fear** – Feeling afraid, anxious, tense, stuck, paralyzed, numb, etc.

Can you remember the last time you felt love? People often describe it as walking on sunshine, good vibrations, or light. Now recall the last time you felt fear. People will describe fear as being tight, tense, numb, or dark.

Can you imagine the difference between how those two emotions feel in your body? We could call these different vibrations. Which of these emotions is vibrating at a lower, slower level? Which end of this continuum is vibrating at a more expansive, open, higher, or free level?

Initially, I was given this list of emotions with no order to it. Later I learned it is even more helpful to view this list as a ladder of vibration, with fear being the bottom of a continuum and love at the top. Imagine each of the seven core emotions having its own vibration.

The first step in developing awareness is being able to identify how and when each of these emotions occurs for you. When you know which of the seven emotions is operating in you, and how to intentionally use that awareness to inform your actions, then you are **emotionally literate**.

## The Emotions Dictionary

When I first heard about emotional literacy and decided to create an emotions dictionary, I began by identifying words that have emotional meaning or connotation for me. I explained what each word meant to me. Then, I began to see how each word could be used to describe one of the seven core emotions.

What are you feeling right now? Which one of the seven core emotions best describes your current emotional state? Close your eyes and ask yourself this question. Take a minute to think about it.

**The Emotions Ladder**

Begin to map your own experiences on the continuum of feelings. Below are some examples of how we may use many words to describe the same emotion. For example, see below how you might use the word *cherished* representing the core emotion of love. Notice how these words group together and represent the same core emotion:

## Love

| | | |
|---|---|---|
| Adoration | Cloud Nine | Liked |
| Accepted | Close | Likeable |
| Affectionate | Compassion | Longing |
| Amour | Content | Nurtured |
| Appreciated | Cooperative | Passion |
| Attractive | Cordial | Relaxed |
| Attached | Cuddly | Safe |
| Calm | Desire | Taken Care Of |
| Caring | Hold Dear | Tender |
| Cherished | Infatuated | Walking on Sunshine |

## Joy

| | | |
|---|---|---|
| Accepted | Flattered | Peaceful |
| Admired | Fortunate | Pleased |
| Alive | Fulfilled | Proud |
| Appreciated | Fun | Satisfied |
| Assured | Glad | Relaxed |
| Bliss | Good | Relieved |
| Cheerful | Grateful | Resolved |
| Determined | Gratified | Respectful |
| Elated | Happy | Thrilled |
| Encouraged | Hopeful | Tranquil |
| Energized | Joyful | Valued |
| Excited | Jubilant | |
| Exhilarated | Loved | |

## Hope

| | | |
|---|---|---|
| Able | Determined | Lively |
| Accomplished | Dynamic | Looking Forward |
| Adequate | Effective | Potent |
| Assertive | Efficient | Qualified |
| Assured | Encouraged | Seeing Possibilities |
| Bold | Energetic | Sharp |
| Brave | Excited | Solid |
| Capable | Fearless | Strong |
| Competent | Self-Reliant | Successful |
| Confident | Goal-Focused | Sure |
| Courageous | Healthy | Together |
| Daring | Intense | |

## Envy

| | | |
|---|---|---|
| Avaricious | Green-eyed | Overprotective |
| Begrudging | Hostile | Possessive |
| Controlling | Invidious | Resentful |
| Covetous | Jaundiced | Rival |
| Distrustful | Jealous | Spiteful |
| Greedy | Mistrustful | Suspicious |

## Sadness

| | | |
|---|---|---|
| Alienated | Dismal | Pitiful |
| Apathetic | Distant | Resigned |
| Ashamed | Distraught | Regretful |
| Burdened | Distressed | Rejected |
| Condemned | Drained | Slighted |
| Crushed | Empty | Sore |
| Defeated | Exhausted | Sorrowful |
| Degraded | Grievous | Suffering |

Dejected
Demoralized
Depressed
Deserted
Despised
Devastated
Disappointed
Discarded
Discouraged
Disgraced
Disheartened
Disillusioned

Helpless
Hollow
Hopeless
Inadequate
Isolated
Lonely
Lost
Lousy
Miserable
Mournful
Neglected
Numb

Terrible
Tormented
Uneasy
Unappreciated
Uncared for
Unloved
Unwanted
Upset
Worthless
Wounded

## Anger

Annoyed
Anguished
Agitated
Aggravated
Abused
Betrayed
Bitter
Coerced
Cheated
Controlled
Disgusted
Displeased
Dismayed
Enraged
Exploited

Exasperated
Furious
Frustrated
Fuming
Hostile
Hateful
Humiliated
Harassed
Irritated
Irate
Incensed
Mad
Patronized
Peeved
Pissed Off

Perturbed
Provoked
Resentful
Repulsed
Rebellious
Ridiculed
Sabotaged
Seething
Smothered
Stifled
Tolerating
Unhappy
Used
Vindictive
Vengeful

## Fear

| | | |
|---|---|---|
| Afraid | Full of Dread | Shy |
| Alarmed | Horrified | Skeptical |
| Anxious | Impatient | Startled |
| Appalled | Intimated | Stunned |
| Apprehensive | Insecure | Suspicious |
| Awed | Nervous | Swamped |
| Concerned | Overwhelmed | Tense |
| Defensive | Panicky | Terrified |
| Desperate | Perplexed | Threatened |
| Doubtful | Reluctant | Timid |
| Fearful | Scared | Tormented |
| Frantic | Shocked | Uneasy |
| Guarded | Shaken | Vulnerable |

## Clarifying Emotional Triggers

Once you have identified *what* you're feeling, the goal is to use that emotion to guide your actions in healthy ways. There are a few steps that will help you to gain this clarity.

Begin by understanding what triggered you to feel what you feel. For example, reading may trigger different emotions. Does reading this book trigger a feeling of joy or excitement? When learning or exploring something new, reading may trigger excitement. Right now do you feel hopeful that you will learn something that will guide you to move forward in your life in a positive way? Or do you feel annoyed or angry because someone required you to read this book?

After I identified words with an emotional meaning or connotation, I then determined the triggers that evoked that particular emotion. For example, when I considered the word *exhilaration*, I noted that I felt exhilarated after exercising, completing difficult projects, and delivering presentations.

Here's my journal entry describing what a few emotions look like for me:

> **Love**: feeling passion about what I am doing or about someone I am with. A blend of excitement, bliss, and wanting the moment to continue.
>
> *Triggers*: Being present to my son, playing with puppies, writing a love letter to my husband pointing out what I appreciate about him, speaking to a group of people who want to learn.
>
> **Joy**: Happy and pleasurable feeling that makes me smile or laugh, feel like singing and dancing when no one is watching, laughing.
>
> *Triggers*: Eating fresh blueberries, greeting my puppies, wrapping a gift and knowing it is exactly what the other person wants, watching my son thrive.

Here is what I wrote in my journal when I heard myself using another word that reflects a feeling and realized for me it was the same vibration level as joy:

> **Exhilaration**: A wonderful feeling that combines excitement and joy. This is the same chemical marinade and vibration for me as joy.
>
> *Triggers*: Finishing a rigorous exercise class, completing difficult projects, delivering a successful presentation that receives a standing ovation from the audience, listening to a client describe a breakthrough as a result of our work together.

## We Are All Wired Differently

After working on my emotions dictionary, I had an epiphany. When someone brought puppies into the office I noticed that while some people *ooohhhed* and *aaahhhed* and melted into a puddle of love, others were clearly annoyed at having their work interrupted. What triggers one person to feel something may have a very different impact on someone else. In that instant I realized that the emotions dictionary that I had been writing, hoping to help people, was a great tool for me but would not work for someone else. This is because we each can use the same words to describe very different emotions. Your brain has 86 billion neurons with several hundred trillion connections between them. This complexity makes you unique because everyone's wiring is different. You and I have different triggers and symptoms when we feel an emotion. Our emotions are unique, like our taste buds.

## Physical Reactions to Emotions

Triggers are just one aspect of the unique wiring in our brains. Physical symptoms of emotions also differ from person to person. Take fear, for example. Speaking in front of a large group can trigger some people to feel fear, but even people with the same trigger will experience that fear differently. Some break out into a sweat, while others have a shaky voice. Still others experience foggy thinking or develop red blotches on their face and chest. People who fear public speaking will experience different physical manifestations of that emotion in their bodies.

Likewise, when you sense danger – perhaps you were almost in a car accident – what do you notice a few seconds afterwards, when you realize you were *not* in an accident? Most people experience a rush of adrenaline that creates what I call "jelly legs," or you may feel the hair standing up on the back of your neck. Different people describe this kind of experience in different ways using their own words. We are not wired the same way when we're experiencing fear.

Coming to the understanding that physical symptoms are unique to each of us helped me to accept that my own emotions dictionary was far from complete if I wanted to share it with you as a meaningful tool for developing emotional intelligence. Consequently, instead of providing you with a complete emotions dictionary, I realized that I needed to provide you with the tools or guide for creating your own emotions dictionary, one that's unique to you.

I also accepted that in order to develop my own emotional literacy, I had to pay attention to how each emotion affected me physically and to then record the triggers along with the symptoms in my journal entries. This is something you, too, will need to do.

Here's how I evolved my understanding of what happens when I feel fear:

> **Fear**: A feeling of perceived danger, threat or harm, a lack of a safety net, either emotionally or physically.
>
> *Triggers*: Perceived loss of value, reputation, title, status, money, or anything that makes us feel unsafe (e.g. a car suddenly swerving toward me, leaning over the edge of a tall building with a fear of heights, or walking alone at night in an unsafe neighborhood.)
>
> *Symptoms*: Accelerated heart rate, inability to think clearly, confusion about what to do next, rapid, shallow breathing, dry mouth, shaking or trembling, with "jelly legs."

## The Other Face of Fear

There is another face to fear that is completely different from the one described above:

**Fear**: Anxiety of not knowing what to do or how to do something, being unsure that you can handle what you've been asked to do.

*Triggers*: Being asked to do something complex, hard or new. Feeling paralyzed by thinking, "I've never been in this situation before," or "I can't handle this. I do not know how to do this."

*Symptoms*: Being confused, overwhelmed, fuzzy thinking, unsure what to do or say next. Wanting to leave or quit, to go watch TV and check-out.

I defined fear in two different ways to point out the varied aspects of the same emotion. Physical danger can evoke very different response from social danger. While I might experience "jelly legs" after almost getting hit head-on by a car, I might not experience the same reaction after being asked by the boss to solve a software problem – something I don't know how to do. Instead of "jelly legs," I might experience a dry mouth or cloudy thinking. Though the underlying feeling for both situations is fear, the physical symptoms can be very different.

Labeling an emotion makes it more manageable according to Seth J. Gillihan, a clinical assistant professor of psychology at the University of Pennsylvania who says, "It does not change the emotion but it does allow us the possibility of choosing our response."

Since we are all wired differently, each person has to become self-aware as the first step in developing emotional literacy. There is no one-size-fits-all emotions dictionary.

Although it looks easy, recognizing your triggers and symptoms can be slow going at first. I know this because there was a time when I was emotionally illiterate and I was unable to easily sort out what I was feeling! I was like Mary, the woman I described earlier, who didn't realize that she was locked in sadness due to her losses.

What follows is a guide to identify your own specific triggers and symptoms as you take the steps to becoming emotionally literate.

## Notice Physical Symptoms

Start by asking yourself, "What am I feeling right now?" Maybe you'll say, "I'm feeling tired." But tiredness is not an emotion; it's a physical symptom. For people who are depressed or sad, these emotions frequently manifest themselves as physical symptoms, including fatigue, lack of energy, lethargy, etc.

Now connect what you are feeling in this moment to the seven core emotions. Notice your physical symptoms and ask yourself again, "What **emotion** am I feeling right now that is expressing itself through these physical symptoms?" It is then that you will understand the impact of your underlying emotions and how they influence your physical health.

## Determine What You're *Not* Feeling

You will find it helpful to go through the seven core emotions and identify what you are definitely NOT feeling. Mary, whom you read about earlier, had an internal conversation that went like this:

"Am I experiencing love or joy? No. Am I feeling anger or envy? No. Hope? Not really. Am I sad? I'm not sure. I'm not crying. Wouldn't I be crying if I were sad? Not necessarily. I think this is the sadness step on the emotional ladder."

Sadness can also be experienced as feeling *blue* or *low*, and though tears may not be flowing, these words all describe the same vibration of sadness.

Someone like Mary, who is not emotionally literate, may struggle to describe the emotion that she's feeling. She may be tempted to say that she's not feeling anything. But the truth is that we are always feeling *something*. Our emotions are always on, whether or not we are aware of them.

## Taking Notice of Your Thought Patterns

By using your emotions as a guide to your actions you are better able to make wise decisions. So how do you identify what you are feeling now and use it as a guide in your decision-making?

Mary is able to see her physical symptoms showing up in her body, such as tiredness, sloppy body posture, etc., but she is not able to see her thoughts. Mary will need to listen to herself and pay attention to what she is thinking and saying. Notice, for example, if there are repetitive thoughts that are circling as if in a loop. What is the nature of those thoughts? Are they uplifting, positive, happy memories, imagined fears, worry, or continually negative images or impressions? Is sensory information processed through a positive lens ("It's fall; the colorful leaves look beautiful!") or a negative lens ("It's fall; the leaves need raking and a cold, dark winter is coming")? Is the glass continually half full (hopeful, optimistic) or half empty (sad, pessimistic)?

By zeroing in on physical symptoms and internal thought patterns, we, like Mary, can begin to pinpoint where we are on the emotions ladder. For example, when you are in a state of love or joy you tend to feel buoyant rather than lethargic, and happy thoughts of pleasurable things fill your mind because that is your focus. Conversely, when you are stuck in sadness or depression, you tend not to have as much energy flowing through you and your mind may remain stuck in a past experience or story of loss. (Recall that Mary had shared the story of her loss in her first meeting with me, even though this had nothing to do with our project together.) We may be haunted by bad memories and thoughts that continually re-trigger sadness, but this can change!

All thought patterns are learned. Keep in mind that you become what you think about most of the time! And we can change our thinking because we have free will. But only we can change our thinking – no one can do this for us. It is a choice we make for ourselves.

Our core beliefs are a choice. They are our repetitive thoughts and they shape our lives, whether or not we are aware of them. To determine your core beliefs, ask yourself these two questions:

1. Do you believe: "If it is to be, it is up to me"?
   Do you see that you have the ability to choose how you will respond to anything that happens in your life? (This is what I mean when I say: see yourself as the predominate creative force in your own life.)

2. Do you think good things happen to you?
   If you pull your perspective back far enough, are you able to see that all is well? Do you believe this is a benevolent universe and things keep getting better and better?

Answer yes to these questions and allow them to become your core beliefs. If you do, then you will create success and joy in your life. What you think about expands. Whatever you believe with conviction becomes your reality.

If you answered no to those questions, it means you are holding yourself back and creating your own glass ceiling. But you can change your thinking! You are the *only* one who can change what is happening in your mind.

Dr. William James, an American philosopher and psychologist who was also trained as a physician, was the first educator to offer a psychology course in the United States. At Harvard, in 1905 he said, "Belief creates the actual fact." He went on to say, "The greatest revolution of my generation is the discovery that individuals, by changing their inner attitudes of mind, can change the outer aspects of their lives."

Later Napoleon Hill, who is famous for writing the book, *Think and Grow Rich*, in 1937 shared this belief when he wrote, "Whatever the mind of man can conceive and believe, it can achieve." But this is not a new idea! Proverbs 23:7 says "as a man thinketh in his heart, so is he."

The truth is you are in charge of your life and your career path – not your boss or your parents. No one else can live your life for you. The greatest enemy of success and happiness is staying stuck in limiting emotions that hold you down, tire you out, and prevent you from creating more joy in the world. You can free yourself from the bad habit of being stuck in limiting emotions by applying what you are learning in this book!

## The Emotional Set-Point

When Mary began tracking her emotions at random points during each day for a month, she noticed a pattern. While she experienced a range of emotions like anger, envy and joy, the emotion that showed up the most for her was sadness. Imagine Mary's emotions as a gauge with the needle briefly bouncing to the left and right, but ultimately settling in the same place, on sadness, most of the time. From this activity, Mary noticed her **emotional set point** was sadness. Mary was a lot like Eeyore, the down-and-out donkey, from *Winnie-the-Pooh*.

Ashley also randomly tracked her emotions for thirty days. She noticed her emotional set point was joy. Although Ashley experienced a flash of anger and a brush with fear, she knew how to handle those emotions. When Ashley felt sad, she acknowledged the feeling and used it in a healthy way to explore what she had lost and what had meaning for her. Ashley was able to use all her emotions to guide her actions; she knew the right questions to ask herself so she would intentionally move back up the emotional ladder and reconnect with joy. I'll show you how Ashley did this as we continue.

## Create Your Own Emotions Dictionary

Now that you've seen what an emotions dictionary looks like, it's time for you to create your own personalized one!

First, choose the mode of capturing your patterns that suits you best. Use this book as a journal or create an electronic document. You may also want to identify a person or a group to discuss this with – a discussion guide is included at the back of this book. Because some of us are verbal learners, we learn by talking things out, so we need someone to be a sounding board for us. Use the discussion guide in the back of this book if you realize you learn best by talking with others about what you are experiencing.

Start by focusing on the seven core emotions. Eventually, you'll see that each of the seven emotions acts as an umbrella for other emotions that are associated with it. For example, the word *exhilaration* could be used to describe love, which is at the top of the emotions ladder. Also, frustration is a form of anger, and grief and depression are extreme degrees of sadness.

Over time, you will create more distinctions in your own emotional vocabulary, just as I did when I made the connection that the word *exhilaration* is the same chemical marinade as *joy* for me. For now, focus on these core emotions:

**Love** – Passion for what I am doing or the person I am with, cherishing, nurturing

**Joy** – Excitement, exhilaration, jubilation, happiness

**Hope** – Willingness to see new possibilities

**Envy** – Jealousy, wishing I had what someone else has

**Sadness** – Despair, longing for yesterday, experiencing loss

**Anger** – Frustration, rage, something or someone has crossed my boundaries

**Fear** – The experience of danger, threat or harm; anxiety about the unknown

# Recognizing Your 7 Core Emotions: Journal Exercise 1

This exercise enables you to apply what you have learned so far. Use the following pages to write your own definition of each of the seven core emotions. Answer these two questions to begin your own emotions journal:

*1. What triggers you to feel the emotion?*

*2. What do you notice physically when you experience that emotion?*

We all experience emotions everyday, but like Mary, many of us drown our feelings and are not aware of them. Completing this exercise over a week will help you raise your awareness of your emotions. The promise of this book is that if you commit to doing the journal exercises over time, you will experience more passion, joy and hope. But remember, you are the only one who can do these exercises for you!

Begin Exercise 1 of your Emotions Journal on the following page.

You may continue reading the rest of the book even if you have not completed this exercise. Please return here when something triggers your emotions.

# Love

## Definition & Examples:

# Triggers:

_____

_____

_____

_____

_____

_____

_____

_____

_____

_____

_____

_____

_____

_____

_____

# Symptoms:

# Joy

## Definition & Examples:

_____

_____

_____

_____

_____

_____

_____

_____

_____

_____

_____

_____

_____

_____

# Triggers:

_____

_____

_____

_____

_____

_____

_____

_____

_____

_____

_____

_____

_____

_____

## Symptoms:

# Hope

## Definition & Examples:

# Triggers:

# Symptoms:

# Envy

## Definition & Examples:

# Triggers:

## Symptoms:

_____

_____

_____

_____

_____

_____

_____

_____

_____

_____

_____

_____

_____

_____

# Sadness

## Definition & Examples:

_____

_____

_____

_____

_____

_____

_____

_____

_____

_____

_____

_____

_____

_____

## Triggers:

## Symptoms:

# Anger

## Definition & Examples:

# Triggers:

## Symptoms:

# Fear

## Definition & Examples:

## Triggers:

_____

_____

_____

_____

_____

_____

_____

_____

_____

_____

_____

_____

_____

_____

# Symptoms:

# Track Your Triggers:
# Emotions Journal Exercise 2

For the next 30 days, track your emotions at least three random times during the day. Set three alarms on your phone or use a cue like a ringing phone or a text message bing. When the alarm or the phone rings, stop and ask:

*"What am I feeling now?"*

Write your answer in this journal and then describe the triggers as well as the mental and physical symptoms that accompany the emotion.

At the end of 30 days, when you review your journal, you will be able to spot the trends and identify your **emotional set-point**.

Begin with what you are feeling in this moment:

# Day 1:
## Emotions, Triggers & Symptoms

# Day 2:
## Emotions, Triggers & Symptoms

# Day 3:
Emotions, Triggers & Symptoms

# Day 4:
## Emotions, Triggers & Symptoms

# Day 5:
## Emotions, Triggers & Symptoms

_____

_____

_____

_____

_____

_____

_____

_____

_____

_____

_____

_____

_____

_____

# Day 6:
## Emotions, Triggers & Symptoms

_____

_____

_____

_____

_____

_____

_____

_____

_____

_____

_____

_____

_____

_____

# Day 7:
Emotions, Triggers & Symptoms

# Day 8:
## Emotions, Triggers & Symptoms

_____

_____

_____

_____

_____

_____

_____

_____

_____

_____

_____

_____

_____

_____

# Day 9:
## Emotions, Triggers & Symptoms

# Day 10:
## Emotions, Triggers & Symptoms

_____

_____

_____

_____

_____

_____

_____

_____

_____

_____

_____

_____

_____

_____

_____

# Day 11:
Emotions, Triggers & Symptoms

# Day 12:
## Emotions, Triggers & Symptoms

# Day 13:
Emotions, Triggers & Symptoms

_____

_____

_____

_____

_____

_____

_____

_____

_____

_____

_____

_____

_____

_____

_____

# Day 14:
## Emotions, Triggers & Symptoms

_____

_____

_____

_____

_____

_____

_____

_____

_____

_____

_____

_____

_____

_____

# Day 15:
## Emotions, Triggers & Symptoms

# Day 16:
## Emotions, Triggers & Symptoms

# Day 17:
## Emotions, Triggers & Symptoms

# Day 18:
## Emotions, Triggers & Symptoms

# Day 19:
## Emotions, Triggers & Symptoms

# Day 20:
## Emotions, Triggers & Symptoms

# Day 21:
## Emotions, Triggers & Symptoms

# Day 22:
## Emotions, Triggers & Symptoms

# Day 23:
## Emotions, Triggers & Symptoms

_____

_____

_____

_____

_____

_____

_____

_____

_____

_____

_____

_____

_____

_____

_____

# Day 24:
## Emotions, Triggers & Symptoms

# Day 25:
## Emotions, Triggers & Symptoms

# Day 26:
## Emotions, Triggers & Symptoms

# Day 27:
Emotions, Triggers & Symptoms

# Day 28:
## Emotions, Triggers & Symptoms

# Day 29:
## Emotions, Triggers & Symptoms

# Day 30:
## Emotions, Triggers & Symptoms

# Identify Your Emotional Set Point by Reviewing Your Past 30 Days: Journal Exercise 3

At the end of 30 days, read your journal to spot the trends and identify your **emotional set point**.

What do you notice about the patterns in your emotions, your triggers, and symptoms?

You want to set your life up so that you live from the top of the emotions ladder (love, joy and hope) at least 80% of the time. How close are you to that already?

_____

_____

_____

_____

_____

_____

_____

## Keep Expanding Your Emotions Dictionary

Once you have created your own basic emotions dictionary with the seven core emotions, keep expanding your journal to include additional shades, variations and nuances of emotion.

As you track and record what you feel and why, notice how your awareness evolves to the point where you are able to not only "read" how you feel, but also become aware of what *others* are feeling.

For example, you may realize your colleague gets red blotches on her face and chest sometimes. What is the emotion that she is feeling when this happens? By being curious about your own emotions, you open up to being curious about other people's experiences and what they are feeling too.

# CHAPTER 2

# Using Your Emotions as a GPS:
# The Questions to Ask
# For Each Feeling

A Global Positioning System, or GPS as it is commonly known, does two things: it shows you where you are and, if you input a destination, it shows you how to get where you want to go taking the best route possible.

In the same way your own internal emotions act as an "Emotional Guidance System" if you know how to use them. If you take the time to map out your emotions, including their triggers and symptoms, you will be able to identify not only where you are now, but also where you would like to go. Then, using your emotional map, you can ask yourself the right questions and take the best actions to get you where you want to go. This chapter will show you how to make it happen.

Your emotions journal is much more than a tool for developing your emotional literacy. As you acquire the skills of emotional self-awareness from Chapter 1 and self-regulation, what you'll be learning in this chapter, your journal tracks your experiences and enables you to learn from your own internal emotional guidance system. Now you will not only know how to identify where you are on the emotions ladder, you will also have a map for moving from the emotions at the bottom of the ladder to the feel-good emotions at the top.

Now that you've identified your triggers for each emotion in your dictionary, developing an awareness of these triggers enables you to either avoid them or seek them out, depending on where you want to be on the emotions ladder.

Ignoring your emotions causes you to move down the ladder. If you ignore your emotions over a long period of time, you become numb to them and you end up being afraid of your own feelings.

An example of this happened one day when, Kim, my intern, told me how being numb, ignoring her body and becoming hungry pushes her down to the lower end of the emotions ladder and robs her of her best self. Her story is an example of what happens when we ignore our feelings:

### Kim's Self-Awareness Story

Have you seen the Snickers commercial, the one where a tough football player acts like a whiny old woman because he is hungry? There is a word for the phenomenon in which congenial people become monsters when they are hungry – and that word is *hangry.*

I would push myself to work and study long hours without taking breaks to eat meals or grab a snack. Then I would lash out at friends and family about the most insignificant issues. Later, when I would reflect on what happened, I was shocked at how easily I could be emotionally hijacked by a well-meaning comment or slight bump in the road if my body was not well-fed. The same is true if I am not well rested.

Once I was able to define how I was feeling and connect it to what I was doing, I was able to make changes in my life. Now I am not numb; and when I start to feel hungry and cranky I notice it and I grab a high-protein snack and take a break to eat – drama and crisis averted!

This is a spot-on example of how being aware of the symptoms early enables you to respond quickly enough to guide your next actions and avoid trouble. By uncovering her connection between hunger and the emotions under the anger umbrella (crankiness, frustration, irritation), Kim now makes a conscious choice to avoid plunging further down the emotions ladder. With a well-timed snack, Kim can keep herself in the upper levels of the emotions ladder, where she is able to maintain composure and focus. When our self-awareness is low, triggers have a way of sneaking up on us and affecting our emotions without us realizing it.

## I Woke Up in the Pantry Eating Doritos!

Did you ever binge-eat cookies or chips without being aware of what you were doing? Binging is a symptom of an emotional state. For me, it's a symptom of fear, but I didn't realize it until I found myself alone in the pantry eating a bag of Doritos without knowing why. This was doubly horrifying to me because I also follow a gluten-free eating plan. And here I was eating a food that I already know makes my body sick. When I tell this story I say, "I woke up in the pantry eating Doritos." But you understand that what I mean is I was not being aware; I was on automatic pilot, and not thinking clearly.

It was at this moment in the pantry when I had this flash of awareness and asked myself: *"What am I feeling now? What am I doing? Is this who I want to be?"* The answer to the first question was fear. My two stepsons were in the living room, fighting with each other. I had an automatic pilot story or a belief going on in my thinking that said: *"There is nothing I can do. When they are in a fight with each other, I can't win. They will not listen to me. No matter what I do, they will turn against me and make me out to be a bad stepmom, just like in all the movies with stepmoms in them."* With that kind of thinking there was no way to create a win for anyone!

I had gotten caught in this limiting thinking that left me numb and unaware of my actions. What's more, my self inflicted, and corresponding physical symptoms had me choosing to eat something that would cause me even more pain. This flash of awareness illuminated what I was actually feeling in the moment, because of what I had recorded in my emotions journal. I was now able to ask myself new questions to change my thinking, such as: *"What do I want to create here? Aren't I the one who serves as an executive coach in corporations and helps executives to resolve conflicts? Couldn't I use those same skills now?"*

With this new awareness, I put down the Doritos bag, went into the living room, and initiated a conflict resolution conversation between the two young boys. The result? The conflict was resolved in a healthy way.

Keep in mind that the same skills we use at the conference room table also can be used at the kitchen table and vice versa.

## Identifying the Patterns in Thinking, Body & Behavior

In the previous story, I recognized the pattern in how fear manifests in my thinking, in my body, and in my behavior. When I'm afraid, a switch gets thrown that creates a "click whirl" pattern like turning on a machine that causes automatic reactions to occur. First my thinking gets fuzzy and I experience confusion about possible next steps or what to say. Then I'm not able to make decisions; papers pile up on my desk because I can't decide what to do with them or where to put them. I also have a tendency to rush myself, or to avoid others and hide in my office – and to eat mindlessly. When I start noticing these actions as symptoms, I know it's time to have a conversation with myself about what I'm afraid of now. I'm not afraid of fear because I know what to do with it! It is nothing more than a guide, a mile marker on my journey.

Sadness, however, sets off an entirely different set of symptoms for me. When I'm sad, I tend to isolate myself and not engage with others even though I feel lonely. I numb out by watching too much TV or shopping online for things I don't need. (How many pieces of green Wedgewood do I really need?) I find myself thinking about getting a new pet, even though I already have 3 dogs. Life feels overwhelming when I'm sad, because I focus on things I can't control or have no influence over. If I'm blaming someone else for my emotional state – or doing any of the other things I've already mentioned – then I ask myself, *"What am I feeling now?"* This helps me to become aware so I can take the right actions to move forward instead of getting stuck.

As you can see through my experiences, by paying attention to changes in your body, thinking, and behavior, you learn to identify an underlying emotion. You then are able to use that awareness to guide your actions. Once you ask yourself the right questions and take the right action, you can begin to move yourself up the emotions ladder.

**Moving Up the Emotions Ladder**

## The Right Questions to Ask for Each Emotion

### The Top of the Emotions Ladder: Love, Joy, & Hope

Whenever you find yourself luxuriating in love, joy, and hope, keep it flowing by asking yourself these questions:

1. What can I do to notice and appreciate this moment, to keep ease and flow going?
2. What am I thinking and what is happening in my body in this moment?
3. How can I milk this moment? How can I continue to enjoy this feeling for myself and expand my experience of joy with others?

## The Uneven Journey Up the Emotions Ladder

The road to your bliss, or your happy place isn't always paved with positive emotions. You will find unexpected twists and turns that take you out of love and joy. And sometimes seeing what we want but don't yet have will trigger envy.

### Envy

Envy, like all emotions, is not experienced in the same way by everyone. For months I tried to find this emotion in myself, but it was not showing up for me. Then, one day a colleague described an experience that sounded amazing to me and I knew immediately that I wanted to add it to my own "That's for Me!" list – my personal list of goals, and dreams, and experiences I want to have, people I want to meet, and opportunities I want to create. Later, as I reflected on it, I realized that this is how I experience envy.

So now, when I learn about something I want to have in my own life, I incorporate that new desire into my own "That's for Me!" list.

On the other hand, one of my clients describes feeling envy as being possessed by a green-eyed monster. She says that envy takes hold of her heart, disconnects her from joy and undermines her best self. For others, envy triggers insecurity and a lack of confidence.

How does envy show up in you? Notice how you react to seeing other people having or achieving what you want. Once you become aware of how envy manifests itself in your thinking and behavior, then use self-regulation to ask yourself the right questions.

When you feel envy, step back and get clear about what you want and what you want to accomplish. Ask yourself these questions when you feel envy:

1. What is it that I want?
2. What action could I take to move myself closer to having that experience?
3. Who could I talk with to get on the best path to achieve what I want?

Use your answers to these questions to guide your actions. Take the steps that become clear as you review your responses. I call this "processing yourself though the emotion." By processing yourself through envy, you can use the emotion to identify what you want to create in your life. As a result, you are able to turn your emotional response to feeling envy into an advantage if you use it to go for what you really want in your life.

The following examples demonstrate how three people responded to feelings of envy. Jasmine, Ken and Kim shared these examples at my Talent@Work® seminar when they attended together.

### Jasmine's Take on Envy

> For me, one of the biggest challenges of being envious is judging myself that I should not be feeling this way.

When we resist an emotion, it persists. The only way to avoid this is to acknowledge what we are feeling. Breathe into it without fear. Allow yourself to be present to the emotion and to see what it is highlighting for you. If you believe, as Albert Einstein did, that we live in a benevolent universe, then look for the good and what you can learn from every situation. If you take this approach, you will use emotions constructively for yourself and for others.

During the seminar Ken shared a very different example of experiencing envy.

### Ken's Take on Envy

> Laura and I started working on the same day in a brand new division of our company. Within a few months, it seemed obvious to me that the boss favored Laura. She was given the best assignments

and I got the administrative leftovers. I felt deep envy when Laura was moved into a private office with a window, while I was still in a cubicle.

Ken is marinating in envy and it is not serving him well, but he does have a choice in how he handles this situation. He can either stay stuck or he can process himself through his emotions to create something better. Ken had a breakthrough in his own thinking when he heard Kim's story during the workshop.

## Kim's Take on Envy

The first time I watched the Victoria's Secret Fashion Show, I started to acquire a green hue. No matter how much I try, at a mere 5 foot 4 inches tall, it is unlikely that I will ever join the ranks of super models like Gisele Bundchen or Karlie Kloss. After realizing this, I figured out how to channel my envy into making positive changes in my life. I want to create the same confidence that the Victoria's Secret Angels radiate when strutting down the runway. I want to feel healthy, fit, and toned, and I want to own a fun, sparkly bathing suit. These goals are all attainable! While it's true: you might not be able to experience exactly what someone else does, but you can create a similar emotional state for yourself. I've learned to ask: *"What is that person feeling?"* In the case of super models, I can imagine that they're feeling beautiful, confident, and healthy. They are enjoying positive attention. Then I ask myself, *"What can I do to make me feel the same way?"* When I aim for the underlying emotional experience, I CAN find ways to create what I want for myself – even if the circumstances don't look exactly the same.

Kim achieved her goals and her story is inspiring!

## Processing Yourself Through Sadness

Sadness can set us back when it appears on our journey to creating more joy in our lives. If your vision of a happy future included a loved one who, through natural causes or life's circumstances, is no longer in the picture, that loss and the accompanying sadness it evokes can help you to understand what you hold dear, value, and love.

Sadness plays an important role by validating our capacity for love. When we feel sad, ask: What is this feeling here to teach me? Sadness points to what you want, what you are passionate about. The loss of a dream, a job, an ability, or a loved one will likely trigger sadness.

When you find yourself marinating in sadness, ask the following questions that will guide you in finding meaning and purposeful action:

1. What have I lost that I was hoping to gain from that experience, person, dream, opportunity, or thing?
2. What have I learned from this experience, person, or dream? What is this feeling teaching me?

3. How can I apply what I've learned to help myself and others in a meaningful way?
4. What action can I take now?
5. What do I want to put on my "That's for Me!" list so that I keep moving forward?

Many people who experience grief turn to purposeful action as a way to cope, so it makes sense to ask:

"What do I want to create?"

Building a memorial garden, establishing a scholarship fund or even volunteering to work with an organization to promote awareness around an issue (such as Mother's Against Drunk Driving) are all positive responses to loss. After losing a job, an emotional boost will come from taking active steps toward reaching a new career goal. Similarly, someone mourning the death of a dream will feel empowered by seeking an even more fulfilling new opportunity.

Consider these two most powerful breakthrough questions when dealing with loss:

1. What could happen in the future that would cause me to look back at this and say that this loss turned into an opportunity that led to an improvement in my life? I am glad it happened, because I am now better (and others are better, too) because I lived through that experience?

2. What action could I take today to successfully move in a positive direction? Acting on this question lets you see that you have choices. You're the only one who can be responsible for your choices. As a result, you are the predominate creative force in your own life.

## Anthony's Story

I was devastated after I received a 360 report – a report that provided anonymous feedback from my board of directors, my direct reports, and a handful of our clients about their experience of working with me. I felt sad, as if the hard work I had been doing was not noticed and people were only focused on my flaws. Physically, I felt as if I had been punched in the stomach. Although there were also pages of positive comments, I kept repeating the negative feedback over and over in my thoughts. I wondered which of my direct reports said, "I do not trust Anthony because he doesn't listen to me and will override my decisions without talking to me." I fretted over who on the board would have said, "Anthony has not explained his vision for the future well enough for us to rally together and bring it to life." And some of the client comments felt like personal attacks. The morning after I read the comments, I did not want to go into the office.

Anthony was enmeshed in sadness. Because he was aware of his feeling, he called me. I served as a sounding board and asked him the questions for dealing with sadness including: "What could happen in the future that would cause you to look back at this and say I am glad it happened, because my company and I are now stronger from the experience?"

As Anthony answered the questions, his sadness dissolved and he became clear about how to use the feedback to help him grow. He decided he would begin to share what he was learning with his team members. He would check in with his colleagues and ask about their experiences of working with him, and listen to their feedback without acting defensively and squashing them.

Anthony accepted that there were gaps in his skills and that he wanted to learn how to grow and improve those skills. He committed to working with me as his coach with a focus on learning how to be a better listener and how to present his vision for the future in a more inspiring way. At my suggestion, Anthony agreed to meet with each board member, look them in the eyes and confirm they were in sync and shared the same goals.

This is new thinking for Anthony, and it reconnected him to what he is most committed to and what he is most passionate about. Out of his sadness, something positive was born.

## Processing Through Powerful Emotions Is a Continual Journey

When dealing with the overwhelming impact of loss, it's important to know that moving forward does not mean never feeling sad again. Sadness comes in waves.

Because my father was ill for a long time before his death, I had already processed myself through deep sadness prior to his actual passing. Others around me expected me to be deeply sad at that time, but for me the sadness came before the death. My father's death marked an ending that in many ways triggered relief for members of my family, who no longer had to see him suffering.

Experiences like the death of a loved one after a long illness, or a divorce, or the loss of a job we hate, are often mile markers that we have already moved through a sad experience, one we may have lived through in waves over a long period of time. Endings in these situations may feel peaceful, and this may not be what others expect us to feel when they hear what has recently happened in our life.

Have you ever noticed when a beloved public figure dies, some people mourn as if they are grieving for a close family member? I call this "proxy grieving." With proxy grieving, we have the opportunity to process any unresolved feelings of sadness over the death of a person we love. This mirroring can happen with any of the other emotions also. It has been clearest for me when I am sad. The unexpected loss of a job or a pet will normally trigger sadness, and with those losses, we may also feel sad about other unresolved issues.

I am reminded of the experience my family had when we were on a long-awaited trip to Paris: the flight was canceled after sitting on the runway for two hours. Because it was Easter break, there were no other flights available for days and we missed our trip entirely. We were sad for days and allowed ourselves to mourn our dream of Easter in Paris. This experience triggered me to relive and let go of other losses that were sad emotions still unprocessed in me.

## Jasmine's Boss & Team Moved On

When Jasmine's favorite boss left her department, the members of her team were moved into new groups. Jasmine was miserable and tears flowed as if she was experiencing the break-up of a deeply important relationship. After asking herself the questions and writing her answers in her journal, she learned that the loss of the boss and the team was not the real issue. She came to understand that she was sad over losing her identity of being part of a high performing team and feeling as if that was now gone.

Once Jasmine realized what was at the core of her sadness, she was able to heal and affirm who she wants to be, no matter what team she is part of; knowing this, she was able to say goodbye to the past and ask herself what she wanted to create next. Jasmine realized that she is a high performing team member no matter what team she is part of because she knows how to process herself and others through emotions. She is not afraid of any emotion now, and that gift enables her to work as a star performer no matter where she works.

But not all relationships have a clear ending. Sometimes we feel sad about the loss of a relationship when someone is transferred to another department, moves away, or is no longer in our daily lives. We may not mourn the loss of these relationships at that time because there isn't a clear ending. For example, around the time of my father's death, images of people I missed whom I did not see regularly any more kept flashing randomly in my thoughts. Because I was vibrating on the level of sadness, the un-processed sadness in me brought up these pictures in my mind and I was able to deal with them.

No matter what the loss, *if you process yourself through the sadness*, your spirits will eventually lift. It may happen in waves, and that is okay. But if you do not process yourself through your sadness, you may get stuck there. Depression is a result of unprocessed sadness. It is not healthy to stuff down or swallow our emotions – they are all there to serve us!

## Make Sense of Your Anger

As with all the emotions, when anger shows up, it's serving an important purpose: it's alerting you that something has crossed your boundaries. To manage your anger effectively, get a clear sense of your boundaries and zero in on who or what has crossed your boundaries. Sound easy? It isn't always easy, especially when you are so angry that you can't think clearly.

Anger can disrupt and derail you, which is why it's important to pay attention to it as soon as it shows up. If you can catch and address anger early, you can prevent it from causing a whole range of negative consequences – everything from the loss of attention and focus, damage to your relationships, and even violence. For example, David Banner is the mild-mannered scientist who transforms into the Hulk when triggered into anger; it's a superpower he dreads because of the destruction it causes. That is how many people think about anger.

A helpful place to start is to learn that there are 3 ways of dealing with anger: passive anger, aggressive anger, and assertive anger. Can you guess which of them is the healthy one?

Can you recognize your own behavior in this list of **passive anger** behaviors?
- Building resentments that lead to manipulation
- Doing something behind someone's back
- Giving someone the silent treatment
- Being secretive or telling white lies
- Making meaningless apologies
- Acting and speaking like a victim
- Missing the real point in feedback
- Being busy and avoiding the big things
- Giving someone the cold shoulder
- Making snide comments

- Being indirect, evasive, vague and projecting blame away from yourself
- Engaging in emotional blackmail, sarcasm, and cynicism
- Letting off steam through sideways verbal abuse and outbursts

Do you exhibit any of these **aggressive anger** behaviors?
- Frightening others with a loud voice or with threats
- Making demands
- Talking over other people
- Using confrontational body language
- Using argumentative or hurtful verbal attacks; name-calling
- Taking anger out on others (kicking the cat syndrome)
- Blaming others and saying things like: "You made me livid…it's your fault I'm this angry!" rather than owning your own responsibility.
- Shouting or using bad manners
- Blocking out or withdrawing from offers of help
- Indulging in mood swings going from not communicating to verbal attacks
- Attacking someone verbally or physically

Lack of emotional awareness and self-regulation can result in both **passive and aggressive anger behaviors**. These are not healthy or effective ways for dealing with an emotion that has the power to wreak havoc on relationships and, in extreme cases, result in violence.

Rather than pouring fuel on the fire of a self-indulgent outrage, it's better to learn a new way of dealing with anger.

In contrast, **assertive anger** is indicative of a high emotional intelligence quotient (EQ), because these behaviors acknowledge the emotion and deal with it.

The following are several constructive behaviors that exemplify **assertive anger**:

- Seeing anger as a signal that something has crossed your boundaries
- Gaining clarity about what you want, what you need, and where your boundaries are
- Having the courage to communicate with clarity and focus about the real issues
- Taking ownership and responsibility for your own feelings and behaviors
- Expressing the need to improve and change
- Balancing words, tone of voice, and body language while saying, "I would like to talk about…" You may also need to say, "I feel strong emotion now and I need to process through this before we talk about it."
- Forgiving and moving on
- Not bringing it up again once you've forgiven, and not carrying resentments

When you're experiencing anger, focus on seeking clarity and determining the course of action that best serves your goals and your relationships. Start by asking:

1. What has crossed my boundaries?
2. Who do I need to talk to about this?
3. Is there value in expressing anger, or would I be better off asking for what I want without focusing on the past?
4. How can I demonstrate assertive anger behaviors in this situation?

When asking yourself the question, "Who do I need to ask to get what I want?" realize that sometimes the person you need to have a conversation with is yourself! You may have crossed your own boundaries by allowing something to happen that is not acceptable to you. Accept responsibility for it and then move yourself forward by creating clarity.

Ask yourself:

1. Do I need to adjust my expectations?
2. How could I do a better job of communicating my boundaries?
3. Where do I want to set the boundary for the future?

It's also useful to consider if there would be value in revealing that you feel anger. You may decide to ask for what you want and need without revealing that you felt anger. Why would you want to do that? Because some people shut down or are triggered into anger themselves when they see that another person is angry. You do not have to reveal the emotion of anger to ask for what you want. Ask yourself, *"Can I ask for what I need respectfully?"* You have the freedom to ask for what you want, but the person who owns the decision also has the freedom to say no. Nevertheless, it's important to ask, because if you don't ask for what you need and want, resentment and fear will build up in you. Resentment is a sign that there are too many times we have ignored our own boundaries.

Finally, in dealing with someone else's anger, it's important to recognize that when people fight, the subject of the argument is rarely the real issue. The argument itself is often the tip of the iceberg, but the real issue is about vulnerability, connectedness, safety, trust and/or love, which are all related to emotional states.

## Robin's Story: Using Awareness to Guide Decision-Making

My team traveled to San Francisco to deliver a major presentation to a client. At dinner the night before, we all agreed that we would meet at 8am in the hotel conference room to set up for our noon presentation, to make sure that all of the technology worked properly and to review each person's role.

We made this plan because previously we had a technology malfunction during a different client presentation and we lost the account because we had not prepared enough. This time, we were determined to learn from our past mistakes and ensure everything went smoothly.

At 7:45 am on the morning of the presentation, I got a text from Joe that read, "Robin, I feel 8 am is much too early to meet. I really need the rest, so I'll be there at 11."

I was furious! My first instinct was to reply to Joe and tell him to get his butt to the conference room ASAP. But then I made myself sit down and think it through before I did anything I'd regret. I asked myself, *"What's the best thing to do for the team?"* I realized that if I lit into Joe and demanded he meet at the agreed time, he would be angry and off his game for the presentation. Delivering an A+ performance was essential, so I took a couple of deep breaths, focused on the bigger picture and decided that I would let Joe show up at 11 am. I would discuss his unacceptable behavior with him on our flight home.

I totally made the right call. Our team knocked it out of the park and we won the account. I also had my conversation with Joe when I could calmly explain why his behavior was a violation of our team work ethic.

## Angela's Take: Setting Boundaries with Yourself

Self-anger can be as big an issue as anger toward others. If you have boundaries about how you are going to treat others and then you treat someone disrespectfully, your anger is a clear signal that you have failed to live up to your own expectations.

Once you identify how you crossed your own boundary, you can make a game plan for getting back on track and making more decisions that align with the image of your best self.

Sometimes the boundaries and agreements we make with ourselves need to be re-evaluated and renegotiated. If you berate yourself for missing an important piece of information in an email, making a typo, or incorrectly entering an event in your calendar then, yes, maybe you could be more attentive. But are your expectations too high? Are they unattainable? Cut yourself as much slack as you would others. When you make the boundaries too weak or the rules to strict, you are setting yourself up to fail. If this happens, it is time to reevaluate and reset your expectations.

## Move from Fear to First Gear... & Get Rolling

If anger is a roadblock that stops you from experiencing happiness and success, fear is a deep pothole. Minor potholes will slow you down; but large ones can immobilize you completely. Nevertheless, the right amount of leverage and momentum can get you unstuck. Fear can be conquered!

Fear is learned and we learn it in two ways. First, we learn fear through experience. (Getting bitten by a dog as a child could trigger you to fear dogs.) Second, we learn fear by observing fears in others. (Seeing your mother shriek at a spider teaches you to fear spiders. Seeing your father fear mushrooms may cause you to avoid all mushrooms.) We can learn fear from our parents, bosses, and team members if we aren't careful.

The important thing to know about fear is that fear can be unlearned and overcome. If you, like me, were bitten by a dog as a child and developed a fear of dogs, you can overcome that fear by having many positive interactions over time with friendly, loving, small puppies and then with larger adult dogs. This is an example of how fears can be eliminated by the use of systematic desensitization and habituation.

The more you know about how fear shows up in your behavior and actions, the better equipped you will be to recognize and handle it before it paralyzes you like getting stuck in a pothole.

### Fear Triggers

Two types of situations trigger fear: when you are either in physical danger or in social danger. Fear can be your ally, alerting you to the need for safety. But fear may be your adversary, keeping you from achieving important goals that could contribute to your success and happiness.

When experiencing the fear of physical danger, the best thing to do is immediately create safety. Slow the car, step away from the ledge, drop and roll, or move from a dark street to a well-lit place.

It's less clear how to handle fear that puts us in perceived social danger, such as when our vulnerabilities are exposed or when we do not know how to do something we think we should. There's nothing dangerous about public speaking and yet many people fear appearing nervous, stumbling over words, or looking bad in front of others.

This is the same type of social fear that comes into play in the workplace when you're asked to do something you don't know how to do. The perceived danger you experience is that others will learn there's a hole in your skill set or may think less of you. Or perhaps you are worried that your boss will question your competence and value. This is the kind of thinking that will trigger fear.

By avoiding perceived socially dangerous situations, we think we are keeping ourselves safe from harm, but instead this type of fear prevents us from growing. We need to learn how to process ourselves through social fear so we can challenge ourselves and grow.

**Process Yourself Through Fear**

To process yourself through a feeling of Fear, ask yourself:

1. Is this the type of fear where I need to slow down or stop what I am doing? (If it is the fear that comes from driving 80mph in a 30mph zone or doing jumping jacks on the edge of a cliff, stop what you

are doing! Don't place the risky bet, sign the unread contract, drink the cloudy water, or do anything else that triggers fear.)

2. Or is this the type of fear that comes from not knowing if I can handle something new?

If it is the second type of fear, start by gaining clarity on exactly what is being asked of you and what you want to know or learn.

Do you want to take on the challenge? Yes! Do you want to learn and grow? Yes! Next, remind yourself that you already have a great track record of successfully learning how to do complex new things. You've learned how to read, drive a car, operate a computer, cook a delicious meal, speak another language, etc. Use positive self-talk as your internal trigger for hope and courage: *"If I can make lasagna, change a tire, play guitar, design a presentation, and raise a child, then I can learn how to do this too! I can do this. I CAN HANDLE THIS!"* This positive self-talk moves you through the fear and up the emotions ladder into feeling brave, hopeful, and courageous.

Identify an expert who knows how to do what you want to do. Learn what she knows, ask questions, read her articles or books. Create an action plan to change your mindset from problem-focused to solution-focused. Why does this matter? In looking at a problem, you are more likely to feel and trigger negative emotions. In looking for a solution, you are engaging with positive emotions, so you are more likely to feel and trigger hope.

Here's an action plan to overcome fear of public speaking:

1. Choose a topic you are passionate about sharing and an idea worth spreading.
2. Read my first book, *Power Presentations: How to Connect with Your Audience and Sell Your Ideas,* which gives you clarity about how to design a talk. Or attend a workshop, and work with a coach who can give you customized feedback when learning this new skill.
3. Write a draft of a talk.
4. Share the draft with colleagues and ask for feedback.
5. Review what you've learned about delivering a speech.
6. Create a practice schedule to be held in a safe environment in front of friends and colleagues.
7. Prepare your own pre-speech ritual: wear an outfit you love, drink a glass of room temperature water with a slice of lemon, reframe your nervousness by telling yourself: "I'm glad I am here! I want to share this information! I am glad my audience is here. I'm excited to be giving this talk."
8. Deliver your talk.
9. Celebrate your successful presentation and overcoming your fear!

Purposeful action is the best way to eliminate worry, anxiety, fear and helplessness. Accomplishing small tasks on the way to tackling larger goals helps you develop confidence and keeps you on the upper rungs of the emotions ladder. Taking action also creates momentum for moving forward–and once you're moving forward, you're not stuck!

The following are several examples of common fears:

## Letting Go of Fear of Speaking Up

Have you ever heard the statistic that the number one fear held by people worldwide is the fear of public speaking? Many people feel anxious at the thought of having to share their expertise in front of groups of people. However, based on my experience, that is not really the number one fear that people carry with them.

What is the most common source of fear? Speaking truth to power and sharing opinions about what is not working well; in other words, addressing conflict with the boss. I could repeat hundreds of stories about well-educated men and women who have told me that they feel shutdown, squashed, and unsure of how to deal with someone who has more power than they do.

Being the boss, team leader, CEO, or project supervisor – these roles all come with a weight attached to them, even before a person steps in to act the part. Why? Because the person in that role has the power to make final decisions on whatever is the area of focus for that job or role (i.e. the project supervisor makes the decision about what the schedule is, and whether you fit into it or not).

As a result of feeling fear, some people have mastered the art of appearing busy and overwhelmed as a way to avoid interacting with the boss. Or they may take independent contributor roles that are highly task-focused to avoid having to engage in one-on-one conversations with the boss. For example, Jane told me that she memorized her boss's schedule to avoid crossing paths with him and potentially being asked questions. Immediately before she ran out the door at the end of the workday, Jane emailed him a report that indicated how many units she had completed.

When you hear the phrase "I was called into the boss's office," what is your first thought? Is it, *"Uh oh, what went wrong?"* Fear of the boss is so common; yet it often surprises leaders to learn that their employees are afraid of them.

Allen, the CEO of a small company, was shocked to learn that his team did not like the way he was handling several client projects. No one had ever mentioned it to him. This was because, on several occasions, Allen felt anger when he learned something was not going the way he'd expected or when not everyone agreed with his decision. In those moments, he yelled and made a spectacle of his anger to the staff. The long-term impact of Allen's behavior was that now no one on his team was willing to share information that they thought would make him unhappy; they were afraid of his lashing out. Although Allen never fired anyone in the heat of anger, when I met one-on-one with each of his employees, each one talked about being afraid that Allen would become so angry that he would fire them. The employees were not sharing very important facts and information with Allen and this lack of communication was holding the company back from growing.

The fear of telling the boss anything perceived to be challenging or uncomfortable is so common, and it severely hinders the creative problem solving that would help both the employee and the boss solve problems together.

What can be done to overcome this common fear of speaking truth to power? People on both sides of the desk need to raise their EQ.

Bosses like Allen can learn how to make it safe for their employees to share bad news and problems, and to offer constructive criticism. Employees can remember that their bosses also want to be star performers in their roles. In addition, employees improve their skill in communicating difficulties by learning to talk to the boss in his or her own style. Knowing how to speak so that your ideas can be heard is a skill that can be learned! It is called "people reading."

If you feel fear about saying what you are thinking, talking about your ideas, or making suggestions to someone in power in your life, the skill you'll want to learn is people-reading so that you feel comfortable speaking to anyone.

This is a skill I teach in *Conversations That Get Results and Inspire Collaboration,* and we will touch on it in greater depth in the final chapter of this book.

## Letting Go of Fear of Failure and Rejection

Rejection and failure are useful parts of life. Just as we learn how to walk, use Excel, or drive a car, we also can learn to be resilient in the face of failure and rejection. You fell many times when you learned how to walk and run, but you did not let that stop you from mastering your goal. Persistence is necessary for success. So next time you fail at a daring idea or your request is rejected, think of it as resilience training! Use the experience to zero in on what you want for your future.

## Letting Go of Fear of Danger

If your fear was triggered by a physical danger, such as a near-miss car accident, you will most likely re-live that fear over and over for a while afterwards. That's because the adrenaline that was introduced to your body during the "almost" moment of impact stays in your body for at least 4 hours. If you allow yourself to feel the fear again by thinking about the incident, you will trigger more adrenaline that will last *another* 4 hours. As the pattern continues, you may feel the effect for days.

It is important to recognize when you are stuck in this pattern, and to make a conscious decision to forgive yourself or others for the near-miss accident. This happened to Kristy Tan Neckowicz, one of the senior consultants with my company, The Professional Development Group LLC. Kristy experienced a near-miss car accident during a drive to Boston. Later that same night, Kristy caught herself restless with insomnia, her over-active imagination playing out the worst-case scenario that could have occurred. She felt afraid and incredibly guilty for putting her entire family in danger. Realizing that she was stewing in the emotion of fear, she made a conscious decision to forgive herself for her role in the incident, and forced her mind to focus on loving and happy moments from earlier in the day and week. By processing herself through her fear, Kristy could more quickly learn from the fear in less time and then get a good night's rest.

## Letting Go of Fear of Judgment

Are you being held back by your fear of judgment? Understand that it is not possible to be close friends with every person you meet. No person on the planet is known and deeply loved by all people. We fear judgment from others even while we are judging others. And sometimes the judgment we feared may not actually exist. We may feel wary of judgment from people who are different than we are–people who have higher positions or seemingly more interesting lifestyles. But in reality, these people may actually want a collaborator or friend. Remind yourself that the most common trait connecting all of us is that of wanting to be loved and appreciated for who we are.

Fear of judgment also can be a red flag. For example, if you fear being harshly judged by a colleague, boss or parent, it could be a sign that you need to move to a more supportive work environment or family. I had to do this myself and know how empowering it can be to recognize when you are in a culture that serves your growth as opposed to when you are in one that squashes and holds you back.

Confront your emotions and ask the questions you need to ask in order to start moving forward. Then take action by focusing on the next highest feeling to proceed up the emotions ladder. Think the thoughts and take the actions that you would take if you were feeling joyful – and soon you will be. Do this without judging yourself and you will experience amazing results.

YOU are in the driver's seat. You choose which way to go – up the emotions ladder or down–and your choices will either speed you toward the destination you've plugged into your GPS or they will slow you down. There will be adventurous detours on your journey, but value them as opportunities to deepen your self-knowledge, develop your emotional awareness, and practice self-regulation.

### Tia's Story of Managing Fear of Change

> Our company was in the midst of a massive internal merger. Change was happening in so many areas and at such a rapid pace that the tensions and stresses were tangible. When your comfortable world is suddenly turned upside down, there is a strong feeling of fear. And when you combine stress, fear, and the unknown, it is easy for panic to set in, derailing all forward progress. At our

quarterly managers meeting, the senior leader asked the group, "How do we get our folks more comfortable with change?"

I had been reading a lot about change management, change motivation, and change leadership during those difficult days. What I began to realize was that the way to get folks comfortable with change is to stop talking about *change*. Our mistake was over focusing on the word instead of what we wanted to create. Change happens every day, everywhere. We wanted to be strategic, so we needed to be agile in our ability to respond to the needs of the market. Inherent in this process is continuous change. But the word *change* incites so much anxiety that it becomes a catalyst for dysfunction.

Instead, I suggested we focus on changing the words we were using in the conversation. So now we talk about strategic agility, and our ability to flex our approach, skills, and communications to fit the needs of our internal customers each day. We've taken the word "change" out of our business vocabulary, and in doing so, we've removed much of the the fear and anxiety attached to the word. Instead, you hear people talking about innovation and creative ideation and flexing department structures and development processes to meet customer and business needs. We are still changing every day, but it feels exciting now!

# Quick Reference Summary: The Questions to Ask Yourself to Process Through Emotions

### Feeling Love, Joy or Hope?
Whenever you find yourself luxuriating in love, joy, passion, and hope, ask yourself these questions:
1. What can I do to notice and appreciate this moment, to keep it flowing?
2. What am I thinking and what is happening with my body in this moment?
3. How can I milk this moment? How can I continue to enjoy this feeling for myself and expand the joy with others?

Living your passions = finding your bliss, happy place, slice of heaven, ease and flow!

### Feeling Envy?
Ask yourself these questions:
1. What did I see that I want?
2. What action could I take that would move me closer to having that experience?
3. Who could I talk with about how to get on a path to where I want to go?

### Feeling Sad?
When you find yourself marinating in sadness, ask yourself these questions that guide you toward meaning and purposeful action:

1. What have I lost?
2. What was I hoping for from that experience, relationship, dream, or opportunity?
3. What have I learned through this experience, relationship, or dream?
4. How can I apply what I learned to help myself and others in a meaningful way?
5. What action can I take now?
6. What do I want to add to my "That's for Me!" list so that I keep moving forward?

If you are sad because of grief, turn to purposeful action as a way of coping. Ask yourself:

"What do I want to create next in my life?"

Then ask yourself the most powerful break-through questions:

1. What could happen in the future that would cause me to look back at this and say that this loss turned into an opportunity that led to an improvement in my life? I am glad it happened, because I am now better (and others are better, too) because I lived through that experience?

2. What action could I take today to successfully move in a positive direction? Acting on this question lets you see that you have choices. You're the only one who can be responsible

for your choice. As a result, you are the
predominate creative force in your own life.

## Feeling Anger?

When you're experiencing anger, focus on seeking clarity
and determining the course of action that best serves your
goals and your relationships.

Ask yourself:
1. What crossed my boundaries?
2. Who do I need to talk to about this?
3. Would I be better off asking for what I want without focusing on the past?
4. How can I demonstrate assertive anger behaviors in this situation?

When asking the question, "Who do I need to ask to get
what I want?" realize that sometimes the person to have a
conversation with is yourself!

Ask yourself:
1. Do I need to adjust my expectations?
2. Do I need to do a better job of communicating my boundaries?
3. Where do I want to set the boundary for the future?
4. Who do I want to talk to about this awareness?

## Feeling Fear?

To process yourself through a feeling of fear, ask yourself:

1. Is this the type of fear where I need to slow down or stop what I am doing? (If it is the fear that comes from driving 80mph in a 30mph zone or doing jumping jacks on the edge of a cliff, stop what you are doing! Don't place the risky bet, sign the unread contract, or drink the cloudy water.)

2. Or is this the type of fear that comes from not knowing if I can handle something new?

If it is the second type of fear, start by gaining clarity on exactly what is being asked of you and what you want to know or learn. Do you want to learn and grow? If yes, remind yourself that you already have a great track record of learning how to do new things successfully. Remind yourself of specific things, like how you've already learned to read, speak a language, drive a car, operate a computer, etc.

Use positive self-talk as an internal trigger for hope and courage: *"If I can make lasagna, change a tire, play guitar, design a presentation, and raise a child, then I can learn how to do this too! I can do this.* I CAN HANDLE THIS!" This self-talk will move you through the fear and back up the emotions ladder into feeling brave, hopeful, or courageous.

Then, identify an expert who knows how to do what you want to do. Learn what she knows, ask questions, read her articles or books. Hire a coach if you need to. Create your action plan. An action plan helps you change your mindset from being problem-focused to being solution-focused.

# Using the Questions to Process Yourself Through Emotions: Journal Exercise 4

Use the following journal space to reflect on when you used the questions you just learned in order to process yourself through an emotion.

If you experience a strong reaction, but did not process yourself through the emotion at the time you felt it, use your journal to work through any unprocessed emotions.

By working through these questions and recording your progress, you will begin to clear out the stuck resentments in your life. The result will be more freedom and the ability to reach higher levels of feeling good. You will be experiencing greater emotional intelligence.

# CHAPTER 3

# Making Better Choices

*Follow your bliss and don't be afraid, and doors will open
where you didn't know they were going to be.*

— JOSEPH CAMPBELL

By now, after using the exercises and techniques in the previous chapters, you have become aware enough of what you are feeling to be able to use your emotions to guide you to make better decisions.

Your GPS in your car provides you with different routes to the same destination based on distance and current traffic patterns. You use the information it provides to choose your path and then make a succession of decisions to follow that path. At any point you can decide to stop for a while or take a detour. Ultimately, how fast you arrive at your intended destination depends entirely on your decisions and choices along the way.

For example, you can decide right now that you want more happiness and joy in your life. And now you have the tools to immediately make the right choices and to practice the right habits that will make you happy. Achieving better emotional well-being is like achieving better physical health. If you have a goal and the determination to have a healthy body, you will make make choices like eating nutrient dense foods, exercising, and allocating eight hours for rest every day. These beneficial choices and practices produce real physical results over time.

Likewise, your Emotions GPS and your new skill of processing yourself through your emotions also provide you with a structure that will help you to create more happiness, love, and joy in your life.

## External & Internal Triggers

To aid in your journey toward making the decisions that bring more happiness and joy to your life, let's dive a little deeper into the importance of triggers. There are two types of triggers: external and internal. They can work together to create an absolutely delightful day or a horrible one. What you do with these triggers makes all the difference in your emotional health.

External triggers are outside of you. You can't control them. A friend stopping by unexpectedly with your favorite food, or receiving a lovely bouquet of flowers at the office, or being invited to a celebration with people you love, are all external triggers to emotions found at the top of the ladder. Other examples include news of an unexpected pay raise or someone at work telling you how you made a positive difference on a recent project.

There are also external triggers that can take us down the emotional ladder. A rainy day might trigger you to feel glum; getting rear-ended on the freeway might trigger anger. Hearing about a terrorist attack can be a significant fear trigger and haunt you for days if you keep re-watching the details on TV.

When you intentionally use your Emotions GPS, you *decide* what to do with an emotion. You consciously revel in or process yourselves through emotions as they show up. When you take charge, you make decisions instead of being on automatic pilot and reacting like a pinball that's bouncing from one trigger to the next.

**Internal triggers** can be controlled because they are your own thought habits. For example, have you ever noticed that replaying a memory can trigger the same emotional response as the event itself?

This happened to Kate. She was getting her teeth cleaned and the hygienist was talking about her trip to Paris. As she described climbing to the top of a bell tower at a cathedral, Kate remembered a time when she ascended a narrow staircase to a great height and her heart started palpitating. There she was, getting her teeth cleaned and in no danger whatsoever, but her body was on automatic pilot, reacting the same way as it did when she was at the top of those steps, looking down and being afraid.

What happens between your ears is just as important as what is happening outside you. What we think about has an impact on us. Our internal triggers are capable of influencing our current emotional state and sending a signal of happiness or fear, regardless of where you happen to be.

Memories are especially powerful internal triggers. Both pessimistic thoughts and positive self-talk are internal triggers. Both can turn into "click whirl" thinking, by this I mean being on automatic pilot when we have the same thoughts over and over without being in control and directing our thinking.

**How do internal and external triggers play off each other?** Consider these three scenarios:

**Scenario One:**
Heidi cherishes her daughter, Julie, and loves her unconditionally. This is an internal commitment she has with herself about her feelings for Julie. She made a decision to act from a place of love for her daughter even in those times when she does not actually feel love.

When her daughter's teacher called to warn her that Julie was struggling in English class and would probably fail the course (external trigger), Heidi initially felt sad and disappointed that Julie had not mentioned this problem to her, and that it had escalated to the point where the teacher had to call to say there was a problem.

Because Heidi made the decision that her love for Julie came first, she was able to create a conversation with Julie to help her to feel secure and cherished first, and then help

Julie create a new plan to learn something that is very challenging for her. Heidi was able to process Julie through her fears of learning something in a new way. Together they were then able to identify a tutor for Julie who could help her to learn what she had been struggling with. Going through this caring, nurturing process made it obvious to Julie how much love her mother had for her.

## Scenario Two:

One Monday morning while driving to work, Dan stops at a yellow light and the driver behind him crashes into his car (external trigger). After realizing he is not badly hurt but that his car is totaled, Dan feels angry. After talking to the other driver, Dan concocts a story in his mind about the guy being an irresponsible jerk, and the story Dan makes up does not serve him or the other guy in any way.

Dan eventually gets to work over an hour late, missing an important meeting. He stops focusing on his anger about the accident and directs his attention to his to-do-list. A few hours later, when his colleague at the water cooler asks, "How is your day going?" this simple question reminds Dan of what happened on his way to work (internal trigger), and after he recounted the story, he feels angry again. At lunch, Dan tells several people about the irresponsible jerk who rear-ended him, and each time his angry feelings return. By the time Dan gets home, he is enraged and rants to his wife about the accident.

Even though it is over twelve hours since the accident, Dan had focused his internal thoughts on the jerk who hit him and was still marinating in those negative emotions because he was internally retriggering himself and escalating his anger.

## A third scenario shows how internal and external triggers play off each other:

Chris's best friend at work, Paul, got fired (external trigger). Although Chris did not know the real reason why the boss fired Paul, it did not stop him from making up a story to fill in the details. Chris's fabricated story was that Paul was fired because the boss is irrational and did not like it when anyone questioned him. (This is an internal trigger; the story you tell yourself to explain why something happened.) Most professionals know that in a work environment it is not acceptable for management to explain the specific details about why a person is let go for poor performance or egregious behavior, but that did not stop Chris from filling in the details for himself.

After convincing himself that his story about the reason for Paul's firing is true, Chris now feels afraid that if he shares his thinking with the boss, he will be fired, too. What Chris does not know is that Paul was fired because he stole something from the company and was caught on video. The HR Director and Chris's boss can't share this fact with the other employees, but Chris's own version of the story is damaging both his relationship with his boss and his work. Chris's "click whirl" thinking does not serve him well.

## Understanding Emotional Hijacks

When we are triggered into an intense emotional reaction, we call that an emotional hijack. Some people might call it a panic attack. We are physically triggered to freeze, fight, or run away. Other physical symptoms of an emotional hijack include pronounced heart palpations, flushing, and shortness of breath. When we experience this kind of intense emotional reaction, we lose the ability to think clearly, and we cannot function at our best.

Mike, the CFO of a small company, was delivering a high stakes presentation to a group of potential investors. A few moments after handing out spreadsheet data, Mike was asked a challenging question about his numbers. Mike looked at the data on the handout and froze. He was not able to think, and a few moments later, Mike left the room abruptly with no explanation. Mike experienced an emotional hijack because, when he realized the numbers on his handout were wrong, he felt an intense rage. He did not know what to do, so he fled.

Had Mike been self-aware, he could have had an internal dialog with himself and prevented his rational brain from being taken over in a freeze, fight, or flight moment. He could have said to himself, "I'm in a hijack and I need to calm myself down." At that point, Mike could have taken several deep breaths, and in the time it would have taken for him to collect the handouts containing the errors, he could have intentionally asked himself the questions necessary to get the analytical part of his brain to engage in creating a solution.

Handling a hijack in a situation like this is difficult, especially for someone who has not practiced processing through his emotions. As a result of this experience, Mike recognized the need to raise his emotional intelligence so that he could think better on his feet and learn how to be a better presenter when challenged. He hired me as a coach and developed the skills for talking himself through moments of panic.

The moment you recognize the signs of an emotional hijack, use self-talk to call it out and move yourself outside of the emotional reaction. Tell yourself: *"I'm in a hijack and I need to calm myself."* Take several deep breaths. These two simple steps will help you to slow down and get out of your reactive state. Then ask yourself the right questions to turn on the analytical part of your brain. If you do not have the list of right questions with you, start with: *"How can I use my ability to think and ask questions to create something better now?"*

Emotional hijacks can linger for hours, days, or even years. As we saw with Dan and his car accident, residual stewing in emotion serves no good purpose. Dan could have processed himself through his anger before walking into his office by asking himself these questions:

## 1. What crossed my boundaries?

The driver of the other car, who was not paying attention and totaled my car.

## 2. Who do I need to talk to about this?

I need to explain to the police and the insurance company what happened so we can handle this.

## 3. Is there value in expressing anger, or would I be better off asking for what I want without focusing on the past?

I can't change what happened. This is one of those situations where I will likely never know the real story about why the other person ran into my car. There is no reason for me to make up a story about it that does not serve me or the other person. No one was hurt – cars were damaged and they can be replaced.

## 4. How can I demonstrate assertive anger behaviors in this situation?

I can ask the insurance company for what I need and focus on finding a new car that will be even better than the one I was driving.

When you find yourself in a situation like this, divert your attention away from the source of your anger, and do not relive the experience over and over through venting or re-telling. Ask yourself the right questions, and then choose only those conversation topics that trigger you to move up the emotions ladder.

When a bad memory creeps into your consciousness, instead of replaying it in your head and letting it derail your day, ask yourself, *"Is there any reason this keeps coming up? Is*

*there anything here I can reconcile now? Am I ready to let it go?"*
Then replace it with more useful thoughts that focus on
something you want to create.

I agree with Ken Rampolla, the CEO of a thriving business,
who says change the phrase "Have a nice day" to "Make it
a great day." We can *make* it a great day when we use
internal and external triggers with the right intention. This
action gives you the choice, and the ability to decide, about
what you want to create for yourself and others. When you
make this conscious choice, you are less likely to be
emotionally hijacked.

**Self-awareness** is the first line of defense against forming a
vicious circle of negative emotions; it enables you to make
choices about how you want to feel.

**Self-regulation** starts a circle of positive emotions. Like
Heidi, making a habit of choosing positive internal triggers
over negative ones makes it easier to bounce back from an
emotional setback. Self-regulation also lays the groundwork
for using emotions as a creative force because you think
better, act better, and work better when you are more
consistently at the top of the emotions ladder.

When you are able to visualize what you want, it puts you
in a place of joy and inspires thoughts of love and hope,
allowing amazing things to start happening for you.

## Love, Joy and Hope: Find Your Bliss, Happy Place, Slice of Heaven, Ease & Flow

Bliss, slice of heaven, happy place, ease and flow – whatever you call it, this is where you want to live most of the time! This is the destination you want to plug into your Emotions GPS! Once you know how to process yourself through your emotions, and you build the internal awareness to do so, you will be able to follow your bliss.

Where is your bliss or slice of heaven? Do you have a picture of it in your mind? If not, then let it evolve – starting now! Are you willing to make a decision today to prioritize your own joy? If so, ask yourself this question:

*"What would my life be like 3 years from now if I were wildly successful?"*

What will you be doing in three years? Write your vision with the details that matter to you. If you are wildly successful, where will you be living? Who will you be interacting with? What will your home and office look like? Imagining your ideal lifestyle can be a positive internal trigger that elevates you out of current frustration or sadness and into action. Reviewing positive pictures in your mind of what you want to create not only triggers passion, joy, and excitement – the internal place where you want to reside – it focuses you on a real-world goal.

If you are not sure where you want to go, that's okay! Sometimes a vision suddenly pops into your head, but it usually evolves over time when you see and experience what you want in your life.

Start paying attention to what you enjoy most. Take action and get involved. When you are doing the things that make you feel most alive, stop and take note. Specifically, what are your surroundings? Are you in the country, in the woods, or in a city? In a library, kitchen, office, or a mall? What are you doing? What's happening in your body?

Take notice of your repetitive thoughts and really pay attention to what feeling good is like in your own body. Sift and sort through your experiences collecting the ones that trigger joy, passion, and love. Track these experiences and work on incorporating them into your daily life and vision of the future. Make it an adventure!

Have you ever noticed someone who seems to have one great adventure after another? Luck or positive serendipity follow this person everywhere. Elizabeth is one of these people. She sees experiences as adventures, and getting a new client is an adventure for her. She creates inspiring adventures for herself and for others, one after another. She focuses on creating happy, joyful experiences and they keep coming into her life.

Once you know what your bliss looks like, create a plan to get there! It will become an ongoing journey to intentionally create based on your passion and what you love.

## Moving Up the Emotions Ladder

You'll know if you are moving up the emotions ladder by the symptoms that start to show up! When you elevate yourself from sadness into hope, and you suddenly see more options and possibilities, notice that your thinking changes from "either/or" to "and."

When you are marinating in the chemicals that go with fear, you are more likely to force yourself into "either/or" choices, as if there are only two options. This creates pressure to make the right choice now, as opposed to giving yourself time to explore options and make the best choice.

When you are operating from hope, you have the ability to see lots of options more easily and you make better decisions after evaluating your options and thinking them through. For example, when I'm feeling sad, I disengage from people; but when I feel hope, I'm willing to connect with new people to discuss ideas. Optimism returns and obstacles suddenly seem conquerable. I start to think, *"Even though I do not know how yet, I know we can figure it out."* I take actions that correspond to what I know triggers more joy, love and passion for me and for others. Once the momentum of positive thinking and feeling gets going, I am able to inspire myself and others.

How do positive emotions like hope show up in your body and mind? Do you notice that your muscles relax, your digestion gets better, and your sleep patterns improve?

Does your thinking seem suddenly clearer, your focus sharper? Is this when your creative juices start flowing with new ideas?

On the other hand, how do limiting emotions, like fear and sadness, announce themselves? Do you notice stomach problems, headaches, back and neck-aches? Are you more indecisive? Do you procrastinate? Is your energy level low; do you constantly feel tired?

You know the answers to these questions when you have high self-awareness. Take note of these signals so you can process them and move back up the emotions ladder. *You* decide what you want to take action on or pursue.

Just as tuning in to the triggers that help you make the best choices will keep you moving up the emotions ladder, so can identifying the symptoms associated with particular emotions help you to continue moving upward. Both of these activities enable you to build overall emotional awareness, which will put you in the driver's seat. *You* make decisions about how you want to feel.

## Self-Regulation

Using awareness of your emotions to guide your choices is a form of **self-regulation**. Self-regulation is the ability to redirect disruptive impulses and to suspend judgment, enabling you to think first, before acting. We've been calling it "processing yourself through your emotions."

Remember Mary who was stuck in sadness? Once Mary had the self-knowledge of her "set point" in the emotions hierarchy, she began to intentionally move herself up the ladder and out of sadness.

Mary did this by creating her own emotions dictionary with detailed entries on love, joy and hope, to help her understand what triggered her into those emotional states. As Mary began to value herself enough – to feel worthy to seek those positive triggers – she noticed that helping others made her feel good and she began to find ways to do that more. Since Mary loved to garden, she consciously chose to work in her garden when she felt her spirits sinking. She now seeks the company of other people who enjoy the same interests. Mary now spends free time doing only the things she loves, and she makes the choice to surround herself with joy. The result is that Mary now values her internal emotional guidance system.

At the same time, Mary consciously minimized or even eliminated what caused her to dwell on loss. Instead of replaying images and thoughts of a loved one in the end-of-days struggle, Mary mentally focused on remembering that person in life, recalling joyful memories of time they spent together. She surrounded herself with uplifting pictures, memories of inspiring moments they shared, and she told stories about good times. Now when she walks her beloved dog, Mary notices the beauty around her. She is making better decisions.

## It's Okay to Feel What You Feel

This is not to say that Mary should stop feeling or expressing sadness or grief. It's ALWAYS okay to feel what you feel. We don't use emotional awareness and self-regulation to deny or suppress any of our emotions.

In fact, when you suppress an emotion, it tends to express itself anyway, somewhere under the radar of your awareness. In other words, emotions can affect your demeanor, your thoughts and your actions without you knowing it! The classic example of emotions "coming out sideways" is when you yell at your dog or snap at your family after having a bad day at work. When emotions "come out sideways," you take it out on someone else, instead of feeling, acknowledging, and using that anger appropriately to fuel you to taking the right actions.

## Identify Your Emotions Without Judgment

A GPS device first locates *you* before it can give you directions on how to get where you want to go. Have you ever heard the gentle voice in your GPS say, "Please make a U turn"? That gentle voice does not judge or berate you for being where you are. In much the same way, begin to identify your feeling without judging yourself.

The act of asking yourself what you're feeling requires that you momentarily step outside the emotion you're feeling, to engage your thought processes. While your Emotions GPS consults with your understanding, and searches for the place where you are standing on the emotions ladder, you are slightly outside of the experience of the emotion itself. In other words, one foot might be firmly planted on, say, the sadness rung of the emotions ladder, while the other is suspended in midair while you decide where to place it next. Now, instead of two planted feet, you only have one. You're already halfway to getting unstuck!

Deciding you want to move up the emotions ladder is the first step in moving up!

## Emotions GPS in Action

Do I want my child or employee to feel fear? Yes! If he is driving over the speed limit or if he is about to walk down a dark alley in an area known for muggings, I want him to feel a flash of fear that keeps him alert or makes him question an action.

You never want to turn off any of your emotions. You'll want to feel fear if you are doing jumping jacks on the edge of a cliff. Fear makes you slow down or stop. Using an emotion to guide your actions is the power of being aware of your Emotions GPS.

## Dave's Story

Dave decided to be more emotionally connected to others because he wanted to form more meaningful relationships. To help him meet this goal, I encouraged him to speak up about what he was feeling and to ask others about what they were feeling.

After doing this for a month, Dave began to feel more confident in his ability to identify his own feelings. He also got better at using his emotions to guide his actions. Dave was also becoming a better listener. He was now listening to whatever the other person wanted to express, without being anxious that he had to act on or resolve other people's feelings. He realized being present and listening intently was enough for others to appreciate him.

About two months into this relationship experiment, Dave called me to say, "The ability to express what I am feeling has helped me to become a better friend because I am being authentic. I no longer feel like I have to be good at everything. I am not judging my emotions as being good or bad. Instead, I am using them as a guidance system and making conscious decisions. As a result, I am better able to listen to others and to ask questions that help them process their emotions too. I'm now feeling more connected to my co-workers and friends."

## Angela's Take: Are You Going in the Right Direction?

During the first week of my emotions journaling, I spent an undue amount of time trying to distinguish between the emotions I was feeling at the upper rungs of the ladder. I felt good but wondered, *Hmm...is this a joyous feeling or is it love?* Or *I'm feeling love and joy, but which one am I feeling more?* That is when I realized that the better question to ask was, *In what direction am I deciding to move?* If I am moving on an upward trajectory, using my GPS to identify my emotions and choosing to process myself through them, then I am making good decisions.

## The Benefits of Using Your Emotions GPS

The decision to use your Emotions GPS and to process yourself through your emotions will inevitably lead you to experience more happiness in your life. And that, in turn, will enable you to be more successful. Why? Because people who are emotionally literate, who choose to make their most significant decisions from the top part of the emotions hierarchy, are better able to:

- Complete tasks faster
- Feel better about their quality of life
- Earn more
- Become star performers
- Influence others
- Suffer fewer career "derailers"
- Experience less stress
- Adapt better to change

Think about it, when you love what you do, you enjoy spending time getting better at it. Then it's not work; it's play! And it is your decision!

**Using Your Emotions GPS**

# Create Your Own "That's For Me!" List: Journal Exercise 5

Begin creating a "That's for Me!" list to focus on the things, people and experiences you want to incorporate into your life. Aim to have at least 100 entries! Include both personal and professional items, big and small goals. Some people call this a "bucket list." Don't put limits on yourself. If you don't let yourself explore and create at least 100 entries describing your goals and future vision for your life, you are creating a glass ceiling for yourself!

## Using Your "That's for Me!" List

Once you are in the habit of using this list to plan your time, you will begin to see that you really are the predominant creative force in your own life. Continue to add to the list as more ideas occur to you about what you want to create.

I challenge my coaching clients to read their own list daily for several weeks and begin to track the significant progress they are making in achieving their goals. Do this yourself and watch what you set into motion that has a positive impact on every area of your life.

Move the items you complete to an "I did it!" list. My coaching clients tell me they feel inspired and excited when they read this list and watch their "I did it!" list grow. Confidence, a sense of accomplishment, and more joy are the result and can become a trigger to guide you up the emotional ladder.

# Create a Love, Joy & Hope Folder: Journal Exercise 6

Create a folder of things that trigger you to feel love, joy, and hope. Include photos, videos, and songs that make you smile. Add documents (thank-you notes, positive emails, great performance reviews, etc.) that remind you of your best self and past successes.

After processing yourself through an emotion, visit this folder as a trigger to help you move up the emotional ladder.

Note a few ideas for your folder here:

# CHAPTER 4

# Living Your Passion

Now that you know how to use your own Emotions GPS to process yourself through negative emotions without being afraid of them, you will begin to spend more time in hope, joy and love.

This chapter will show you another way to use your Emotions GPS to follow your bliss. Instead of inputting the destination yourself, you will let your emotions guide your path. Once you have developed a high emotional awareness, you will be able to use it to uncover activities, assignments and roles that are connected to your passions. You will begin to notice that opportunities and things light up in new ways as they trigger your path to expanding love and joy. When your passions are engaged, you're happy because you are doing what you love.

## What Motivates You?

Have you ever experienced being so engrossed in an activity that you were surprised at how quickly the time passed while you were doing it? On the flip side, have you ever watched the minutes of a clock slow to a crawl when you were forced to do something unpleasant or uninteresting?

When I'm coaching clients, teaching seminars, or working on a new presentation, I disappear into time and get so focused that I even forget to eat! But when I spend a day doing administrative tasks and cleaning out junk email, lunch can't come soon enough!

Pay attention to the moments when you are blissfully unaware of the passing of time; noticing this will guide you toward what you value deeply. Tune into the environments where you feel most alive or sense a deep connection. Intentionally create more of these experiences.

My friend, Sophia, notices an energy surge when she enters a library or a bookstore. Everything about that environment speaks to her – from the rows of books neatly organized on shelves, to the sense of calm and quiet so perfectly suited for reading, to the distinctive way books smell. This same energy comes over her when she's in a school or on a college campus; she feels twenty years younger and ready to enroll! Why? Because she loves learning, so she's naturally attracted to objects and places of learning, like books, schools, and libraries.

On the other hand, when Sophia visits a mall, she feels as if her senses are under assault. Department store perfumes hang too heavy in the air; music pulses loudly in every space, and seemingly endless displays of merchandise compete for her attention. While some people might love seeing all the fashionable clothes, accessories, and beauty products, Sophia is overwhelmed by them. Clearly, Sophia does not connect with the mall environment. It would not be wise for her to choose to work in this type of environment because it would signal an undervaluing of herself and her unique combination of talents and abilities.

What you value at your core both attracts and motivates you. What you don't value struggles to engage your attention. Values and motivators are the same thing. By tuning into your emotions, by noticing what makes you feel most alive, you use your Emotions GPS to guide you toward your values and motivators. This leads to meaningful work, relationships, and soul-satisfying play, all of which are the source of true joy.

## The Six Motivators

Just as it was helpful to identify the seven core emotions and use that framework for developing self-awareness and self-regulation, it is also helpful to understand that there is a similar framework of motivators. But keep in mind that, there is no hierarchy – one motivator is not better than another.

According to the research of Eduard Spranger and later G.W. Allport in *The Study of Values,* there are six basic values or "motivators." There is no value judgment associated with the order in which they appear. Here are the six basic values or motivators, in alphabetical order:

**Aesthetic** – Wanting things to be artistic, creative, subjective; striving for balance, harmony, and peace.

**Individualistic** – Wanting to be part of leadership decision-making, striving for the highest level, and being seen as the best.

**Social-Work** – Wanting to benefit and help others, putting other's needs above one's own, solving people problems.

**Theoretical** – Wanting to find solutions, learning, using facts and data, and sharing knowledge.

**Traditional** – Wanting rituals, guidance in how to live or work in the best possible way; having operations or traditions to pass onto others.

**Utilitarian** – Wanting things to be practical, useful, productive, and financially sound; keeping score, perhaps with points, numbers, or money.

Each of these motivators is present in everyone to varying degrees. You have a motivator to a greater degree when it drives you toward action and shows up over and over in the things you do, the topics you talk about, the places where you prefer to spend time. When you have a motivator to a lesser degree, you're indifferent to those things or experiences; or, if the motivator is really low, you're driven to avoid them entirely. Experiences that repel you are typically reactions to your lowest motivators.

Do you recall Sophia who loves books, schools, libraries, and learning? Can you identify which motivator is high for her? If you said the **theoretical motivator,** you're correct!

She clearly loves acquiring knowledge, seeking truth, solving problems and doing research. If you give her an assignment that involves any of these things, she will happily work for hours until fatigue or hunger stops her. She doesn't need to be offered a carrot or be threatened with a stick to do a good job because she's naturally driven by the pursuit of knowledge. No wonder she feels at home in books, schools, and libraries!

Someone else, on the other hand, might have a very low theoretical motivator, which does not mean that they don't like to learn or they don't value knowledge but it does mean their low theoretical motivator drives them to trust their own *intuition,* rather than to rely on research, facts, or data.

Remember Sophia's experience at the mall? Sophia has a lower **aesthetic motivator**. Someone with a *high* aesthetic motivator likes to create things that satisfy a deep connection to beauty, order, and harmony, such as a great outfit, a meal paired with the perfect wine, a perfectly decorated room, or a musical or visual composition. While Sophia may appreciate those things, she does not readily notice them and they don't drive her to action. When her aesthetic motivator is really low, Sophia insists on things that are functional rather than harmonious or beautiful.

Every one of us possesses a unique combination of motivators, and that is what forms our core drivers. In other words, the WHY for our action is born out of our motivators.

These six motivators are not right or wrong, good or bad. They have no morality. It is how we use them that determines whether or not they are used ethically or not. Every one of these six motivators has the potential to be used for good or for bad – in ways that lift others up or tear others down.

Consider, for a moment, two surgeons. One has high theoretical and individualistic motivators, so she's driven to use research to invent new therapies and to be the best in the field. Another surgeon has high social and utilitarian motivators, so he wants to find the most efficient way to help the greatest number of people. Motivators will not guide us to know which one is the better doctor.

## Identifying Your Own Motivators

Let's return to Sophia. She has already discovered her high theoretical motivator because she's been paying attention to how she feels in bookstores, libraries, college campuses and learning activities. If she keeps following that process, a second motivator also will reveal itself.

To help Sophia in her journey to understand her passions, I suggested that she reflect on the following questions:

### 1. How do you spend your free time?
Examples: volunteering, reading, investing money, pursuing a business goal, making crafts, hiking or enjoying nature, etc.

## 2. Where do you spend your money?
Examples: going to concerts or restaurants, supporting charities, buying craft supplies, supporting a tradition you believe in, seeking educational opportunities, etc.

## 3. What places do you gravitate toward?
Examples: churches, museums, nature, restaurants, urban centers, concert halls, office buildings, etc.

## 4. What topics do you love talking about?
Examples: Politics, religion, arts, entertainment, business results, investing money, sports etc.

## 5. What tasks associated with your job do you like doing the most?
Examples: researching, managing spreadsheets to track a dashboard of data, creating policies and procedures, training others, serving customers, etc.

When Sophia answered these questions, she noticed that she spent a lot of her free time volunteering in various ways; she chaired an outreach committee for her church, raised her hand to mentor new employees at work, and fostered dogs while helping them find forever homes. When a neighbor asked her to tutor her son, Sophia agreed but struggled to set a price for her services. She would have gladly done it for free. (Clearly, she's not motivated by amassing wealth – an indication of the high utilitarian motivator!) In conversations, Sophia loved talking about books and took enormous pleasure in recommending them. The only thing Sophia loved doing more than learning was *sharing* what she learned to help others.

### Sophia's Second Motivator

In addition to theoretical, can you guess Sophia's other top motivator?

If you guessed, social-worker, you are correct! When Sophia reflects on where she derives the most pleasure, she identifies her core passions and puts them on display for anyone who is observant and intent on discovering what makes Sophia "tick."

When you develop an awareness of what drives you, then you are better able to recognize what drives others. Being able to discover what drives the people around you is a very important skill for building relationships and collaborating with others. Whether you're a leader, a parent, a family member, a friend, a co-worker or a manager, there will be times when recognizing someone else's passions means the difference between inspiring them or stifling them.

### Patricia's Story

After attending my High Performing Team Retreat, where her team discovered their motivators, Patricia brought this point alive as she shared a story about caring for her elderly mother:

> My mother had a very high aesthetic motivator. I never would have realized this if it hadn't been for

your coaching. After we discussed motivators and how to recognize them in others, I started to understand my mother's behaviors and began seeing them in a whole new way. Before, I would get frustrated with my mother when she kept pestering me about hanging her pictures in her new assisted living apartment. I also ignored her constant requests to take her shopping. 'You'll get tired, Mom,' I would tell her. But the opposite was true. My mother was never more energized than when she was decorating her apartment or shopping for a new outfit. I am so deeply grateful that I could recognize, finally, that creating order and beauty was what gave her joy. From that moment on, I didn't see her behavior as nonsensical, annoying, or risky for her health. I knew that it would trigger her to feel happy.

## Dan's Motivators Dilemma

Dan's father, Mark, inherited a family business that had been thriving for several generations when Dan began working for the company. The family business made and sold safety equipment for manufacturing companies. Just out of college, Dan was expected to sell all the various types of safety products. His goals were clear: to identify and grow new business with manufacturing companies.

As is typical, the company culture mirrored that of Mark, its CEO. His top motivators were utilitarian and traditional. Mark rewarded employees for doing things in practical ways, and being efficient with money while following the systems and rituals that were passed down from the operations team. Mark's lowest motivator was Social-Worker, so he rarely thought about his business as a venue for helping people. Mark donated money at the end of the year by writing a check and did not think much about or appreciate community events or helping people in meaningful ways.

Nine months into the job, Dan floundered in his work and was not meeting any of his goals. Mark brought me in to coach Dan because it was clear he was not thriving. Dan had not brought in new customers and was instead deeply involved in helping existing customers without charging for his services, something that frustrated Mark when he realized how much time Dan had been spent in this way.

Only ten minutes into my first private conversation with Dan, his eyes welled up with tears and he told me that he was working very hard. He wanted to help customers and still please his father, but he was not clear on how to do so. He felt sad because he thought that not meeting his father's expectations meant that he was not succeeding in anything.

I had Dan complete an assessment on the spot. It revealed Dan's top motivators were social-work, individualistic, and theoretical in that order. What do you think Dan would be most excited about doing?

When I asked Dan to tell me about what he was proud of from his past, he talked about leading several sports teams to winning state championships and how he created playbooks to share with team members to help them memorize plays. He also mentioned his involvement as a Boy Scout troop leader and how he led training sessions to help the scouts collect more food for the local soup kitchen. Dan had also been part of a team that opened a new soup kitchen in his community and he showed me the story that had appeared in the local newspaper highlighting his efforts. Dan's girlfriend worked for the United Way and he shared several activities that they had recently done together which were meaningful to him.

As I taught Dan and Mark about the motivators and debriefed both on their assessment results, they became clear that they were judging Dan's motivators as bad or ineffective, instead of playing to his strengths in helping the family business. After a few weeks of coaching Dan to guide him to track what inspired him and to help him to see how his motivators could add value to the family business, a new role was created for Dan that played to his unique strengths. Dan met with all the existing customers to explore how to create new products to help their employees do their jobs better and determine the services they needed, as well as provide feedback on how they could become the leaders in their market space.

After three months of asking these questions, Dan saw a niche in the market and realized that offering safety training would be a great add-on service to his company's existing product line. Safety training for new employees would be a meaningful way to help people. Dan designed a safety training program for employees who would be using his company's equipment. Dan collaborated with a master trainer to learn how to lead that training.

A year later, Dan's training programs proved to be a profitable service offering for his family's business and Mark was thrilled that together they had turned things around. In fact, Mark's perception and appreciation of his son had grown so much that he gave Dan permission to spend five days leading free safety training sessions to unemployed people in their community through a United Way program!

## Your Motivators & Your Internal Emotions GPS

Awareness is the key to setting yourself up for success and happiness. Once you know what makes your senses come alive, your brain will fire with new ideas, and your body will hum with energy, and you will then begin to choose and to seek out those activities.

Even better, you will clearly communicate with others about what brings out the best in you and ask for what you want. Eventually, you will begin to naturally apply this same awareness to creating deeper connections and more satisfying relationships.

This is not to say that you won't encounter disappointment or experience failure. You still will feel sad sometimes. Those experiences are part of life, learning, and growing. But once you know what brings you joy, once you've followed your bliss or found your happy place, it's easier to find it again when you lose your way. When you input a place you've already been to, your GPS remembers and retrieves the directions more quickly. It's the same with your internal Emotions GPS. You will also use it to find higher levels of joy and passion than you have ever experienced before.

# Identify Your Top Motivators & Opportunities to Use Them: Journal Exercise 7

Read through your emotions journal to find the activities that trigger you into hope, joy and love. Organize these activities into the six motivator categories.

Notice the patterns: where do most of your positive triggers show up? Those will indicate or reflect your top motivators. Use the following journal pages to explore this question:

How could you begin to raise your hand for assignments and opportunities to do more of the things that align with your top motivators?

# CHAPTER 5

# Focusing Outward

*Happiness is never something you get from other people.*
*The happiness you feel is in direct proportion to the love you give.*

— OPRAH WINFREY

It is now time for you to make the shift from focusing internally on what is happening between your own ears to focusing outward on what is happening in your relationships with others. The first part of developing a high emotional intelligence quotient (EQ) is all about understanding yourself. Master that, and then use it to focus outward and understand your emotional impact on others.

## Your Emotional Wake

Have you ever been on a boat and looked behind it as it moves through water? What do you see in the water behind the boat? You see the boat's wake, which is churning and frothing water pushed out of the way as the boat moves through it, creating waves as it passes. We do the same thing in our relationships with each other.

Can you think of someone you'd be excited to see if she were walking down a long hall towards you? That excitement is evidence of a **positive emotional wake**.

Now can you think of someone you'd want to make a U-turn to *avoid* if you saw her coming down a long hallway towards you? That aversion is a sign of a **negative emotional wake**.

Track your emotional wake with others to begin to understand your relationships:

1. With whom do you have a positive emotional wake?
2. With whom do you have a negative emotional wake?

The antidote to a negative emotional wake is to begin creating positive experiences in the ratio of at least 5 positive emotional experiences to one negative. This builds a positive emotional bank account in the relationship. For a relationship to grow and thrive, we must have significantly more positive experiences than we do negative ones.

Anne has a story that illustrates how you can intentionally turn the tide on a negative wake. Imagine how you might apply this same kind of thinking and behavior in a work setting to build rapport and create positive emotional wakes with colleagues:

### Anne's Story

I have found that my feelings follow my actions. When I'm annoyed with my husband, I can give into the feelings, which I often do, or I can do something very kind in response. I have noticed that if I choose to take the high road, my husband reacts to my kindness and I feel better about him and subsequently raise my own vibration.

For example, I was holding on to some negative feelings about incidents that had already been resolved over the weekend but that had left behind a negative wake for me, so I decided to leave some short grateful notes around the house. One read, "Thanks for working so hard to support our family." Another read, "Thanks for working out at the gym and taking care of yourself." I left a note by the dog food container saying, "Thanks for being a great 'daddy' to our 5 pups throughout the years." I let go of my anger and he responded in many positive ways throughout the day. He even cleaned up the kitchen that night, a task that is generally mine.

Now I'm feeling great about him and he's feeling the same way towards me. When I find myself going back and thinking about how angry I was a few days ago, I switch those thoughts off and instead begin thinking of all the good things he has done. My feelings followed my actions of kindness and showing gratitude.

Gary Chapman, in *The 5 Love Languages*, identifies Acts of Service, Affirmation, Gifts, Shared Time Together, and

Touch as the ways we can create positive experiences for others.

Notice what works for you. What is a positive emotional deposit that someone else makes with you? What are examples of deposits you make into your emotional bank account with the key stakeholders in your life?

## Kate's Story

One day I opened up my inbox and saw an email from my son's English teacher. "Oh, no!" I thought to myself. "This can't be good."

The email began with: "Back in September, I asked your son: 'If you ever do anything really well in my class, whom would you want me to tell?' He said he wanted me to tell his parents."

The teacher went on to detail how my son had done an excellent job on an oral presentation. I was floored. Usually, I only receive communication from school when things are going badly. I was so awash in gratitude for this positive communication that I immediately wrote the teacher back and thanked him. And, at the end of the year, I wrote a letter to the principal, telling him of my positive experience with this English teacher.

With that one email, this teacher made a significant deposit into my emotional bank account, and he did the same for my son. Three years later, when this teacher applied for an assistant principal position at another school, he asked both my son and me if we would agree to be interviewed by the hiring committee. Of course we agreed. He had created a positive emotional wake with both of us, we were only too glad to speak on his behalf!

## Empathy

Chris, a dentist, was running late. He had hit the snooze-button on his alarm clock twice and then his dog threw up and he had to clean up the mess before he could leave for work. He hated being late and his thought pattern that he created because of it went like this: *"I'm late. I did not prepare well enough and now I am screwing up the schedule for the whole day. This will affect everyone all day. I hate days that start like this."* He repeated this over and over as he swerved through traffic trying to make up for lost time. This, in turn, created tension in his upper body and back, which made him appear stiff. His anger at himself was evident when he walked in the door to his dental office.

Chris was not aware of the story he was creating. He carried this emotional wake with him because he had not processed himself through his feelings. The repetitive stories we tell ourselves create an emotional wake in all our relationships including the one we have with ourselves.

Joyce, his receptionist, said, "Chris, I realized you were stuck in traffic so I moved your second appointment to later in the day when you had an opening. It's going to be okay. Is there anything else I can do for you to help lighten your mood?"

Joyce was demonstrating empathy in action. **Empathy** is our ability to identify what the other person is feeling in the moment and to be present to that experience with him or her. When we are highly empathetic, we are able to help someone else process his or her emotions as a result of our deep listening and well-executed questions.

Can you think of a time when you have seen this done well? Become observant so you can be empathetic. Notice what another person is feeling and respond to it in a helpful, conversational way. Track your experiences of both being empathetic as well as receiving empathy from others.

## Emotional Social Skills

Intentionally creating a positive emotional wake with others and using empathy to build strong relationships are examples of what I call **emotional social skills**.

Take a minute to reflect on mentors in your own life. Who were the people who brought out the best in you? How did they inspire you?

These are the kinds of things we say about people who inspire us:

- She listened to me.
- He understood how to use my strengths.

- She was growing and sharing what she was learning with me and the team.
- He was passionate about what he was doing.
- She gave me confidence; she believed in me.
- He was focused on solutions.
- She built trust over time.

Now ask yourself these questions:

- How can I do more of these things in my own relationships with others?
- How can I be a better listener?
- Do I notice other people's strengths and affirm them for what they do well?
- Do I focus on solutions?
- Do I make it safe for people to share what they're thinking – even if I disagree with them?
- Have I built up enough trust so that when I do provide constructive criticism, it's clear that my intentions are to nurture growth, not thwart it?
- Do I live at the top of the emotions ladder and exude love and joy most of the time?

We have all experienced positive mentors, just as we have also encountered negative people who discouraged us. Take a minute to reflect on someone who had a negative impact on your growth. What did they do that caused you to disengage or feel squashed?

Usually, this is what we say about people who squash us:

- He was critical and judgmental.

- She seemed exasperated, frustrated, angry or annoyed most of the time.
- He was aloof and distant – unwilling to engage.
- She was self-absorbed.
- He was controlling; it always had to be done his way.
- She focused on problems and blaming others.
- He did not seem to care about me or understand my strengths.
- She complained to me about other people.

Now ask yourself these questions:
- Am I doing any of these things?
- Who can give me honest feedback on whether or not I have these behaviors?
- Am I unpleasant to be around because I live in the bottom half of the emotions ladder most of the time?
- Am I mindful of how others might be feeling?
- Do I tend to blame others for my own lack of achievement or success?

You may discover that you have relationships in which you function as an inspiring mentor and others where you fall short.

Remember me eating Doritos in the pantry? In my professional life I help executives navigate conflict and yet I felt fear about doing the same for my stepsons. Thankfully, I challenged myself and applied these same emotional social skills I use with clients to engage my family members more positively.

The same thing can happen when you work in a team. You may feel a strong connection with six of your seven direct reports who are flourishing under your leadership, but not with the seventh, who seems stuck in a negative dynamic. It may be that this team member needs something different from you. Use your emotional social skills to listen, process, and adapt as needed to create a healthier connection.

Whenever you create positive interactions with others, you are using emotional social skills. These skills show up in your ability to connect and form relationships, to organize others and build networks, to navigate conflict and foster collaboration.

When someone has well developed emotional social skills, high performing teams emerge in their wake.

Remember Ashley from the first chapter? She was able to bring a group of people together and have them collaborate, focus on and deliver results toward a common goal. Being in her presence feels exciting and inspiring; in other words, Ashley has a positive emotional wake that energizes her team, brings out the best in them, and inspires them to grow. She is a mover and a shaker because she has big goals for herself and her team.

## Finding the Right Path

When people say, "Follow your calling," they really are telling you to follow your joy because it will take you to clarity about what your natural talents are and how you can bring them alive in the best possible ways.

Your calling, your ability to expand love and joy in the world, will serve you and others in meaningful ways. Dr. Martin Luther King Jr. once said, "Greatness is determined by service."

How can you serve your way to greatness? You can do this by following your own emotions to live at the top of the emotions ladder most of the time. Have the courage to follow your joy. You will lift your life up to your highest calling only by following your emotions up the ladder.

How do you know if you are on the right path? You feel it! No one can tell you what your path is; only you can feel your way. "Does it spark joy?" is the question Marie Kondo uses in *The Life-Changing Magic of Tidying Up* to help readers determine what to keep. Only items that spark joy remain.

 The same is true for what we do, how we use our time, and with whom we spend it. "Does it spark joy?" paves the way to follow your bliss, to find your calling, to serve others in a meaningful way, and to achieve the highest levels of success.

When you are asked to do something for which you feel no enthusiasm or joy, that's a sign. Your spirit is speaking to you through your emotions. Listen to it.

Who or what do you cherish? When you approach someone with deep feelings stirring in you, you trigger something in them, too. New possibilities open up as a result. When you make it obvious that you cherish a child, a friend, or a colleague, you uplift vibrations that extend beyond you. Love is all around if you make the decision to focus on it, give it, and live it in action.

On a fall day surrounded by trees covered in amazing orange, yellow and red leaves, I can feel them vibrating love. When I eat fresh blueberries, I can feel them vibrating love. Soaking in a hot bubble bath, I can feel the water vibrating love. When I have the opportunity to deliver a presentation on emotional intelligence to an eager audience, I feel joy vibrating. When you make joy and love the story of your life, it ripples everywhere. Energy vibrates through all of your life.

Below are the internal thought patterns or affirmations of a person who has very high emotional intelligence, who is vibrating at a high level, and who is able to focus on collaborating with others in ways that are meaningful.

Look through the list and select several that speak to you. Rewrite and claim those specific affirmations and read them daily for 60 days to make these thoughts a habit in your automatic "click-whirl" thinking.

## Choose Your Affirmations:

- I am clear on my goals and how to collaborate with others to bring good things to life.
- I know the truth is that I have high ideals, integrity, and respect.
- Only good comes from me.
- I maintain a positive and optimistic outlook on life.
- I know that each adversity has opportunities for me to learn and grow.
- I feel grateful in every moment for my expanding awareness.
- As I grow, so does the world around me.
- I am able to relax and let ideas bubble up in my mind to guide me.
- I handle success with love and joy.
- I am willing to accept emotional intelligence to maximize prosperity for myself, for all the people I know, and for all humanity.
- Prosperity includes emotional and physical health, peace of mind, and financial well-being.
- I now claim prosperity in all forms.
- My prosperity cannot be limited.
- There is only abundance available now.
- The perceived lack of resources is the cause of many of the problems in the world today and I choose not to go in that direction for myself and my team; we focus on creating solutions.
- No person, no thing, no event can keep the positive good from me that this loving supportive universe has waiting for me.

- I dissolve in my mind any thought that doesn't serve me.
- I am worthy of releasing the old fears and anger from my past.
- I review what I am grateful for and list my blessings daily.
- I have many blessings.
- I believe there is a seed of value and strength in every human being.
- I develop that seed of value and strength in others by focusing on it, talking about it and encouraging it.
- I have harmony in relationships; all my relationships are in order.
- I am willing to put forth the effort to bring my greatness alive.
- I am guided by my emotions and I listen to them understanding they are communication to me from my soul.
- I move into harmony with the universe and I open my mind to receive abundance in all areas of my life.
- I feel my unlimited potential.
- Flashes of thought and clear plans begin to appear in my mind and the path lights up as I use my emotions to guide me to expanding love and joy.
- I clear out the unused, unnecessary thoughts and things that no longer serve me.
- Opportunities unfold for me and I move in harmony towards them as they light up a realization within that I am in ease and flow.
- I am open to receive.

- I am attracting to me, like a magnet, the relationships, things, and experiences that I visualize and desire.
- I open my subconscious mind to new levels of love and joy.
- What I focus on expands and I experience love and joy easily.
- I dissolve in my mind any thought that is limiting me, and I release it now.
- Goodness is streaming to me and I love sharing it with others.
- I open my mind to receive joy.
- Health, peace of mind, joy and love are the thoughts that I focus on.
- I easily let go of the worn out things, relationships, and experiences that keep me from joy.
- I feel myself receiving good.
- The things from the past that triggered me into emotional hijacks can no longer impact me because I decide what I will think about.
- At this moment I can feel prosperity on all levels.
- I am able to forgive things past, present and future.
- I mentally affirm that I forgive all who have offended me from the past.
- I choose to forgive anyone and anything that needs forgiveness. I am free and they are free, too.
- All things are being cleared up between me and anyone with whom I've had challenges, now and forever.
- All things are cleaned up from my past and my present because I make the decision now that this is so.

- I recognize that I live in an abundant universe and that love prospers.
- In my daily time set aside to listen to myself, I feel guidance from my soul and the infinite intelligence that is within all things.
- I turn my thoughts to the vibration of love and I see abundance all around me.
- I cultivate the thoughts of love, life, joy, and abundance and I see the loving universe around me.
- I have a right to be here now.
- I have a right to enjoy and to love.
- Whatever limitations I experienced in the past are dissolved and move out of my life now.
- I immediately dissolve negativity and let it go.
- My mind dwells on peaceful harmonious thoughts.
- I have a steady flow of good things coming to me.
- Every day in every way I am growing and getting better and better.
- I see symbols of increasing abundance all around me.
- I receive in love and abundance.
- Self-confidence is mine.
- Failure is only defined by my reaction to it–I choose to see mistakes as opportunities to learn how to do something better.
- Everyday passion speaks to me through my feelings; I am listening.
- I have the right to change my mind, to change my thinking, to change my beliefs.
- I am conscious that doors are opening for me in new ways because I am expanding my capacity to feel love and joy.

- The good of all concerned is taken into consideration in ease and flow as I make decisions.
- There is a river of joy and love flowing to and through me.
- I open my mind to prosperity and I am receiving joy, passion, love.
- Money is a means of exchanging energy, of exchanging love.
- Money is energy in a form that enables me to use it to bless everyone and everything in my world.
- I bless everyone with whom I come into contact with my thoughts and actions.
- The love and joy I desire for myself, I desire for everyone.
- I want everyone to have and enjoy this awareness so I share it freely with others.
- Abundance is everywhere; if I look to see it, it will show up.
- I project and share my prosperity with everyone through love and joy.
- Everyone and everything that crosses my path experiences increased prosperity – we are gifts to each other.
- I make the time to say "Thank you" many times each day and to let myself feel the blessings around me.

## These Are Beliefs That Will Enable You to Grow!

Please share your story with us or ask a question. Please email us at The Professional Development Group LLC at **info@YourTalentAtWork.com**.

# Summarize Your Learning: Journal Exercise 8

Now go back through your journal and read it from the beginning to the end. Take time now to summarize your learning.

How have you benefitted from applying these ideas?

Notice your growth and how you have evolved over the past 30 or 60 days, now that you know how to focus on developing your emotional intelligence.

Write yourself a letter or talk with a friend sharing how you have grown. This helps you to anchor your experience.

Take notice. Your life is a journey of learning to love yourself so that you can create more love and joy in the world.

# Book Discussion Guide

In the introduction to this book, I compared emotional literacy to foreign language literacy and pointed out that fluency in both "languages" can be achieved through focused effort and determination.

When learning a foreign language, there are often classes, assigned reading and writing exercises, and due dates to provide external motivation for focusing on this skill.

A weekly or monthly book group can offer a similar structure for those who want a place to process their learning with others and also provides a timetable for completing journal entries.

Start your own group by identifying up to 6 people who are interested in raising their Emotional Intelligence Quotient (EQ). These can be co-workers, family members, friends — whoever would like to join you in a journey of self-discovery and self-mastery.

Agree to tackle one chapter per meeting and to complete all journaling associated with the chapter.

Use the questions on the following pages to guide your discussion:

# Chapter One: Getting Ready to Thrive Becoming Emotionally Literate

- Who are the people you enjoy being around? Do they tend to be more like Ashley or Mary? What is it about them that makes their company enjoyable? What common attributes emerge from your discussion?

- Choose an emotion from the seven core emotions and compare personal definitions with each other. Are there differences in how you all have defined this emotion? Why is it important to note these differences?

- Has tracking your own emotions for 30 days made you more observant of how emotions show up in others? What is the impact of this new awareness?

# Chapter Two: Using Your Emotions as a GPS: The Questions to Ask for Each Feeling

- What stories in this section really spoke to you?
- What stories helped you process through an emotion?
- What is the most difficult emotion to process? Discuss this as a group. Do you all agree on the same one?
- Share a story about how you processed yourself through an emotion.

# Chapter Three: Making Better Choices

- In what ways have you been empowered to make better choices after reading this chapter?

- How can you use your "That's for Me!" list as a trigger?
- Think about the vocabulary you have acquired for describing your emotional experiences (emotional set-point, internal and external triggers, emotional hijack, etc.). Has this new vocabulary contributed to raising your Emotional Intelligence Quotient (EQ)? Why or why not?
- Once you're clear about your own triggers, do you think it's possible to identify someone else's triggers? Why or why not?

## Chapter Four: Living Your Passion

- How does having insight into your own motivators help you connect with joy?
- How does recognizing other people's motivators help you improve your relationships with them?
- How do our motivators impact how we define success?
- How might our motivators impact what we listen for in conversations? In meetings?
- What do you think are your personal motivators? Why?

## Chapter Five: Focusing Outward

- Share examples of people who have positive emotional wakes. What actions help them generate such a positive wake?
- Think of someone who might experience your emotional wake as negative. What are some specific

actions you can take to change your emotional wake from negative to positive?

- Discuss how you might use empathy to change someone else's negative emotional wake.
- Why is empathy associated with effective leadership?
- If you benefited from this discussion group, invite 6 more people and create a new group! Keep the learning going!

# Continuing the Journey!

## Congratulations!

If you did the activities, wrote about your own experiences, and shared your learning with a discussion group, you have grown. You have begun to build skills that will last your lifetime, be useful wherever you go, and transform your life and relationships for the better.

## Keep Learning

If you would like to experience deeper learning with others in a workshop format, consider attending Talent@Work®. Our seminar will take your understanding about building meaningful relationships much deeper. You may also sign up for the Your Talent@Work® newsletter by going to our website: **www.YourTalentAtWork.com**.

# About the Author

Shawn Kent Hayashi is the founder and CEO of The Professional Development Group LLC, Executive-in-Residence for the Lehigh University MBA Program, and a global expert in developing collaboration and high performing teams.

Shawn is a dynamic speaker and executive coach with deep experience working in entrepreneurial companies, Fortune 500, and associations around the globe. Her practical strategies, anecdotes and real world solutions are highly relevant in business today. Shawn delivers keynotes and unforgettable closings customized to conferences or corporate meetings.

Shawn's TEDx talk on The Future of Talent@Work presented her optimistic view of coming changes to the workplace.

As an executive coach and high performing team consultant, Shawn facilitates growth in leadership ability, emotional intelligence, communication skills, stronger relationships and teams, and effective presentations. She guides leaders to achieve positive, lasting changes in behavior – for themselves, their people and their teams.

She is also the best-selling author of the Conversations Trilogy: *Conversations for Change, Conversations for Creating Star*

*Performers,* and *Conversations That Get Results and Inspire Collaboration.*

Shawn earned an M.S. in Organization Dynamics from the University of Pennsylvania. Learn more about Shawn at **www.YourTalentAtWork.com.**